I REMEMBER SOUTHIE

All-in-all, the essence of I REMEMBER SOUTHIE is as the title infers — millepede bits of historic memorabilia, reveries rainbow tinted. True history in memoriam appreciative of the sacrifices our forefathers made in laboring to erect and maintain home, religion and governmental institutions. And, also, by the God-given right of our inheritances there is included an intent that we continue along that illustrious path once trodden by our parents.

I REMEMBER SOUTHIE

Text and Original Illustrations

By

LEO P. DAUWER

A BOSTON BICENTENNIAL CELEBRATION

THE CHRISTOPHER PUBLISHING HOUSE
BOSTON, MASSACHUSETTS 02171

*A Joyous, Illustrated "Bicentennial Guide"
to South Boston's Past, Present and
Future Which the Author-Artist, Among
Others, Places as Forever*

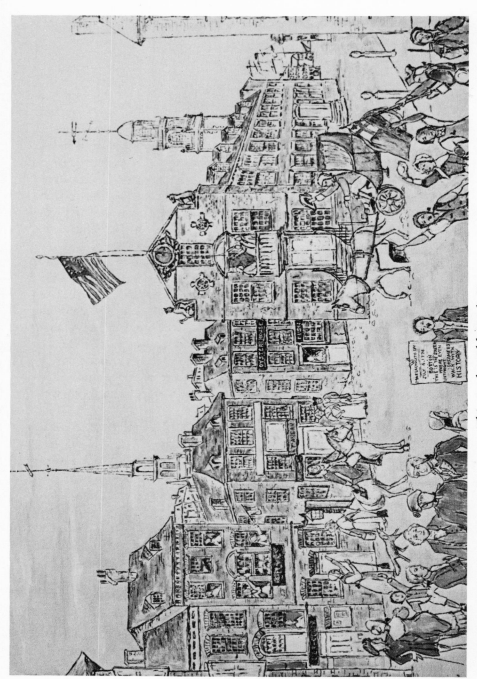

This Is the Old Brick Town

PREFACE

Two centuries have passed since that memorable Saint Patrick's Day, March 17, 1776, when Washington's cannon, perched high on a South Boston hillock in a test of courage, forced the British Army to evacuate Boston to the rebel Brahmin who, in turn, a half century later through the onslaught on their ballot boxes, vacated the venerable peninsula with all its Yankee traditions to the fast gathering, home-seeking immigrants.

The advantages of South Boston's site for its first European settlers was apparent. It was, and still is, a narrow neck of land connected to Dorchester and Boston Proper—a sheltered harbor on one side, deep enough to float ocean-going vessels and a small inner bay on the opposite shore (Dorchester Bay) safe for the accommodation of small fishing and pleasure craft. The peninsula was a countryside suitable for grazing, farming and orchards; it had abundant timber for construction and firewood, and plenty of fresh water in the several ponds and a running stream that finished its course at Indian Powwow Point (at the foot of K Street).

There is no going back in history, no Wellsian time flying carpet to transport us magically back to the early decades of the 1800's in South Boston's rootings. The expanding industries that had sprung up since the Civil War made a sign that rural South Boston was passing. The harborbound peninsula suddenly had become a booming phenomenon of mansions and tenements, wharves and ships, churches and graveyards. Pensive historians thought South Boston's changing decades gay, some rather somber. Most, however, agreed that they were both prosperous and bleak, fastidious and crude, kind and cruel. But art and memorabilia can take us back there to relive at least some of the precious moments vicariously, and that is what is undertaken in the gathering and assemblage of the Boston bicentennial saga —

"I REMEMBER SOUTHIE"

7

ACKNOWLEDGMENTS

The acknowledgments are intended to prevent the necessity of frequent and formal allusions, in the course of the following pages, to the sources from which the information they embody has been derived.

My appreciation for research assistance extended by Librarian Marjorie M. Gibbons, South Boston Branch Library District: *A History of the Community,* Washington Village Library District, 1963, M. M. Gibbons.

For research assistance extended by the Boston Public Library, Copley Square, Boston, Mass.: Newspapers in microfilm.

For the privilege to explore and photograph for illustration purposes, the innermost chambers of Fort Independence, Castle Island in Boston Harbor, courtesy of Captain A. A. Swanson: historian Metropolitan District Commission, State House, Boston, Mass.

For the material relative in part to Fort Independence, Castle Island, Boston Harbor, Edward Rowe Snow, Marshfield, Mass.: *The Islands of Boston Harbor.*

For statistical information relevant to the famous *L Street Bathhouses,* South Boston, Mass.: former superintendents, Robert "Bob" Donovan and Leo Russell.

To reprint statistical material relevant to Boston firefighters, "Bob" Foley and "Ken" Bruynell, Boston Fire Department.

For material pertinent to the career of James Brendon Connolly, South Boston athlete and winner of the first Gold Medal awarded at the First Olympic Games in Greece, 1896: Fred Alexander, Pocasset, Mass.

For material relevant to the career of Benjamin V. Drohan, South Boston songwriter and show business personality: Mrs. "Marty Drohan: in behalf of Mrs. Drohan, Mr. William McCarthy, Roslindale, Mass.

For material relevant to the *Beatty, Santoro and Walker Memorial,* Leonard J. Walsh of South Boston, Chairman of the Memorial. Ac-

knowledgment thereof to the parents of the three deceased boys, all
of South Boston:

> Mr. and Mrs. Richard J. Beatty
> Mr. and Mrs. Ernest Santoro
> Mr. and Mrs. Theodore A. Walker

For material from the publication *My Country 'Tis of Thee,*
American Tract Society, Oradell, New Jersey: obtained through the
courtesy of the Rev. Paul E. Toms, Park Street Church, Boston.

For anecdotes relative to early day semi-professional football in
Boston: Mr. William McCloskey, Whitinsville, Massachusetts.

For material relative to the historic Union Oyster House in Boston:
Mr. Richard L. Greaves.

For material in part relative to Thompson's Academy on Thompson's Island, Boston Harbor: from the book *The Four Thompsons:*
Historian Raymond W. Stanley, copyright 1966 by Thompson's
Academy.

For material from the *Newsletter,* volumes 1 and 2, relative to
Thompson's Academy and for the privilege to visit and photograph
for illustration purposes, the island and buildings: Headmaster Mr.
George Wright, Thompson's Academy.

For the material relative in part to Gillette Safety Razor Co. newsletter dated August 9, 1960; also the pamphlet *Historical Background
on Factory Area:* Gillette Park, South Boston.

My thanks to Mr. Walter C. Fannon, Public Relations, Gillette
Safety Razor Co. for providing the author-artist with the short
Horatio Alger-type story of the inventive genius of King C. Gillette;
The Conquest of the Beard who gave to the world a safety razor that
revolutionized men's shaving habits the world over; quotations are
from an original article by Mr. Gillette in 1918, to which added data
in 1925 was appended.

The poem, "St. Patrick's Day": reprinted by permission of
Lawrence Burns, Swampscott, Mass.; published in the *Boston Globe,*
March 17, 1969.

The lyrics of the song, "Southie Is My Home Town"; composed by
Benjamin V. Drohan, South Boston, Mass., "For good and valuable
consideration"; the non-exclusive, non-assignable permission to print
in the United States the lyrics, "Southie Is My Home Town"; copyright 1935 by Santly-Joy, Inc.; copyright renewed 1962, and assigned
to Joy Music, Inc.; renewal copyright assigned to Anne-Rachel Music
Corporation.

1876, George E. Ellis, Boston, A. Williams & Company, Press of Rockwell & Churchill, City Printers.

Illustrated History of South Boston, compiled by Bancroft Gillespie, Inquirer Publishing Company, 1900, issued in conjunction with and under auspices of The South Boston's Citizens' Association, 1901.

For material relating to the original South Boston Savings Bank building, the Perkins School for the Blind, Castle Island and the shipbuilding industry in South Boston, a special word of gratitude go to the South Boston Savings Bank, its president, Alfred W. Archibald, and the Robert J. Seamans Advertising Agency for their outstanding historical series entitled "The Great History of South Boston."

CONTENTS

ILLUSTRATIONS

I REMEMBER SOUTHIE

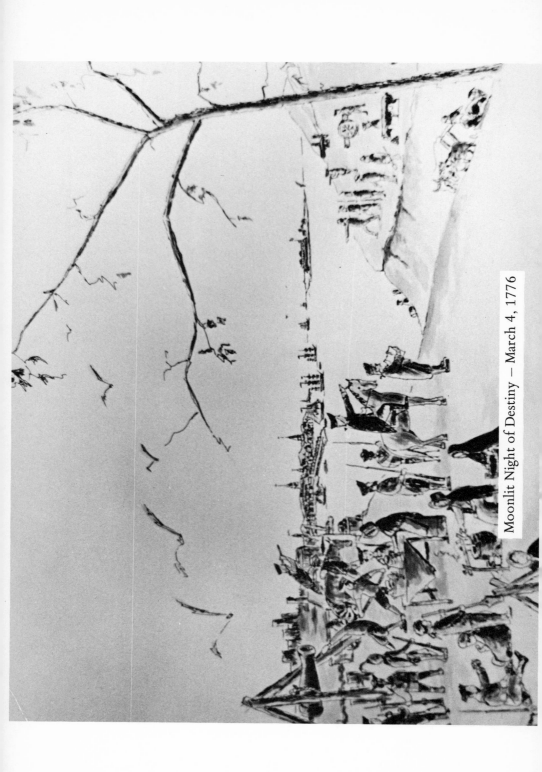

Moonlit Night of Destiny — March 4, 1776

MOONLIT NIGHT OF DESTINY

(circa March 4th, 1776)
Dorchester Heights, South Boston

Generals Washington and Thomas, looking down from the upper-most heights of the South Boston hillock on a clear moonlit night of March 4th, 1776, saw the little surrounding peninsula only with the scrutinizing eyes of aggressive and determined soldiers. Northwesterly, below and beyond in plain view of the plotting generals a cannon-ball distance away and clearly discernible against the evening sky were the "crisp silhouetted church spires and roof tops of the be-sieged Boston Towne."

Washington's hill-top ramparts were reinforced by heavy cannon Henry Knox had secured at Fort Ticonderoga, and which had been hauled by men and oxen over difficult wintry terrain. It was because of the strong fortifications at Dorchester Heights that the British troops under General Howe were eventually forced to evacuate Boston by ship on March 17, 1776.

The intangible contribution of colonial women to the success at Dorchester Heights was as significant as was their material aid. When the farmer or rural mechanic dropped the tools of their calling to shoulder a musket, the womenfolk dutifully picked them up to finish the task. Besides laboring on the farm, women capably admin-istered to the absent soldiers' business affairs: whaling, inn-keeping, shipping, buying and selling of commodities. Wives of the departing tradesmen became shoemakers, cutlers, coach builders, netweavers and bricklayers.

Legend tells us that when urgency was required, a Massachusetts housewife was capable of an early morning to clip a pastured sheep's wool, have it carded, spun, woven, dyed and stitched into trousers readied to adorn her volunteer's backside by late evening. And when the soldier lad was warmly clad, the mother took down the musket from over the fireplace, pointed him in the direction of Dor-chester Heights and tearlessly admonished him to behave like a man.

19

The works on Dorchester Heights of South Boston were constructed with a view of forcing the enemy to attack the American lines. On the 26th of February, 1776, Washington wrote: "I am preparing to take a position on Dorchester Heights, to try if the enemy will be so kind to come out to us."

On the 23rd of August, 1775, the work of fortifying Lamb's Dam was begun, the line of fortification was advanced to a point a little south of the present Northampton Street. Lamb's Dam extended from about the junction of Hampden and Albany streets to a point near the present Walnut Place. It was originally built to keep the tide from overflowing the marshes. The works were completed September 10, 1775, without opposition from the British, although within musket-shot of their advanced posts.

The main line of the British fortifications crossed the Neck between Dedham and Canton streets. The works mounted twenty guns of heavy calibre, together with six howitzers and a mortar battery. The main road leading to Boston passed directly through the centre of the works and was closed by barrier gates.

The works on Dorchester Heights were constructed on the night of the 4th of March. The works commanded both the inner harbor and the town of Boston, and left the British but one alternative, either to evacuate Boston, or to drive the Americans from their fortifications. The latter course was determined upon and twenty-four hundred British were ordered to rendezvous at Castle William (Castle Island) for the purpose of making a night attack on Dorchester Heights.

A furious storm arose; the surf was so great upon the shore where the boats were to have landed that they could not have lived in it. The attempt was abandoned, a council of war was held and Sir William Howe determined to evacuate Boston.

A MONUMENT TO A MOMENT
OF A GREAT DECISION

(Hallowed Ground)

On top of Dorchester Heights, pointing in the direction of ethereal eternity, stands the symbolic finger dedicated to General George Washington's moment of a great decision. Dedicated on March 17, 1902 on a glorious Saint Patrick's Day - Evacuation Day hometown celebration, the white marble Washington Monument from the platform to the top of the vane is about one hundred and fifteen feet. On this hallowed hillock, the monument commemorates Washington's first Revolutionary War victory in forcing Lord Howe's English lobsterbacks and a thousand Tories to evacuate Boston Towne forever and a day on March 17th, 1776.

The oration by Senator Henry Cabot Lodge at the dedication was held in the newly built South Boston High School in the shadow of the monument.

I like to think of that scene of the dim hidden lights flaring fitfully in the gusty wind, of the men piling up the earth and digging out the trenches with the darkness hanging over them, the roar of the covering guns sounding in their ears, and along the lines the stately figure of the great leader passing by, the joy of coming battle stirring in his heart. Here, on this spot we raise a monument which shall serve as a beacon light to guide future generations to one of the memorable scenes of our history. And here, under its shadow, we can rear a still better monument to the men of the Revolution by the resolve that we, too, will toil even as they did, in darkness and in light, with victory over the present, with deep faith in the future and with abiding loyalty to our beloved country ever dominant in our hearts, ever master of our lives.

From atop the monument, beyond and below, Boston Harbor's historic Fort Independence on Castle Island and Thompson's Island,

A Monument to a Moment of a Great Decision — Washington Monument

first explored by Captain Miles Standish of the Plimoth Plantation in 1621, presents a marine picture book panorama. Gazing inland, and still within "cannonball distance" Boston Towne presents a high-rising silhouette where in 1776 only a few church steeples dominated the scene. At the base of the edifice, all Boston celebrates Evacuation Day each March 17th, commemorating General Washington and his rural militia.

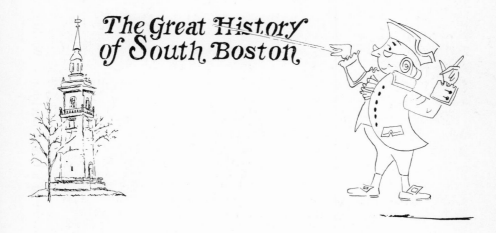

The Great History of South Boston

THE WASHINGTON MEDAL

On March 17, 1876, services were held in the Music Hall in Boston celebrating the Centennial Anniversary of the Evacuation of Boston by the British Army, March 17th, 1776. Prayer was led by Rev. Dr. Manning, Pastor of Old South Church; introductory remarks by Mayor Cobb. Reception of the Washington Medal and a chronicle of the Siege of Boston was given by George E. Ellis, D.D.

Seemingly, the entire country will find interest in the commemorative relics bicentennial to the Evacuation of Boston, 1776-1976 and the heroes of the War of the Revolution. But the cataloguing of ancient memorabilia would not be complete without the key emblem commemorative of the first great victory of the Revolutionary War that occurred on Dorchester Heights in South Boston, March 17th, 1776, Saint Patrick's Day.

The gold medal presented to General George Washington by Congress, for his services expelling the British forces from Boston, remained in the Washington family for a hundred years. In December, 1875, it was purchased from Mrs. Ann Bull Washington "from whom with proper certificates and vouchers, by the generous co-operation of fifty citizens of Boston, it has now been secured to the permanent ownership of this city, with which it is so gratefully identified, and has been deposited in the Boston Public Library." (See page 26, *The Evacuation of Boston 1776-1876,* A Williams & Co., Publishers, 1876.)

Between the date of March 25, 1776, when this gift was bestowed by a resolve of Congress, and the year 1786, by votes of the same body, a series of ten more gold medals was struck at the Paris mint, substantially under the direction of Lafayette. The French Government presented a set of these in silver, including also one in the same metal, to George Washington. This series of eleven, known as the "Washington Medals," finally came into possession of the Hon. Daniel Webster, and, soon after his death, into the hands of his friend, the Hon. Peter Harvey of Boston. This gentleman, in April, 1874, most generously bestowed them upon the Massachusetts Historical Society, in whose cabinets they are treasured. Thus, all the "Washington Medals" are now in the City of Boston.

LONG WHARF

(circa 1950)

Long Wharf, Atlantic Avenue, Boston

T Wharf, the old fish pier, was originally a part of the Barricado of 1672. The neck of the T connecting it with Long Wharf is of that structure. With the fleet of fisher boats moored at its side, it was the most picturesque of all the wharfs along Atlantic Avenue. Its animation has passed with the shift of fishing interests to the then new docks of the great Commonwealth Pier on the South Boston side of the Boston Harbor.

Long Wharf was the aristocrat of the line. It was projected in 1707, when the flats of the Great Cove had been filled on King Street to about where the Custom House sits today. At first called Boston Pier, in time it became Long Wharf because it was supposed to be the longest wharf on the continent. Daniel Neal thus described it in 1719: "a noble Pier, eighteen hundred or two thousand Foot long, with a Row of Ware-houses running so far into the Bay that Ships of the greatest Burthen may unloade without the help of Boats or lighters."

Here the main body of the British troops embarked for the Bunker Hill Battle on Breed's Hill; and, also, the departure of the army of General Howe and the Royalists at the evacuation of Boston on March 17, 1776. A large quantity of stores was left behind on the wharf, and General Gage's chariot was taken from the waters of the dock. A brigantine, a sloop and a schooner were scuttled and left there by the hurriedly departing British.

The British chose the Puritan Saturday evening, the midnight and the early hours for their hasty departure. Howe finished evacuating Boston, leaving the refractory towne. Officers, men and their women-folk in numbers totalling nearly nine thousand, plus eleven hundred Tories, departed in seventy-eight ships. The harbor was not wholly opened until the provincials, by works constructed on headlands drove away the last sentinel ship two years after the Port Bill had closed it.

Long Wharf — A Hasty Departure

The historic Custom House block on Boston's Long Wharf waterfront has been restored and designed into a unique retail-office-apartment complex. The unusual brick lobby with its broad walls of glass, the wood interior of the automatic elevators, the lush carpeting and discreet lighting of the halls with their ancient brick arches and old beams combines early nineteenth century architecture with that of today's modern complex designs.

Boston Towne's high-rise, modern-day skyline, at whose base ancient wharves squat, does by no means form an incongruous silhouette. The harbor with its broad expanse absorbs vessels, wharves, buildings and ocean into a complete maritime panorama. It is here that the sea, the ships and the people have so gallantly contributed to the history of the centuries to give Boston its proud heritage and most treasured traditions.

James Freeman Clark states in his *King's Handbook of Boston Harbor:* "Every sunrise in New England is more full of wonders than the Pyramids, every sunset more magnificent than the transfiguration. Why go to the Bay of Naples when we have not yet seen Boston Harbor."

The windjammer *Spray* of Boston is a replica of the first ship to be sailed around the world by a lone sailor, Captain Joshua Slocum on its sightseeing cruise through inner Boston Harbor. U. S. Coast Guard approved motor vessels with all safety features sail from historic Long Wharf to the outer harbor, passing Castle Island, site of Fort Independence. The history of the various harbor islands and points of interest are narrated by the Captain.

"Here Comes the Parade!" — South Boston's Day

SAINT PATRICK'S DAY

Today's the day for marching if you're Irish
At least a bit of wearing of the green
And the roaring of the Shannon in a man's heart
As he dances with a girl from Skibbereen.

Her eyes look up with all the Druids' magic
And cast their spell from here to Donegal
Wherever Irish men have died for freedom
Who would not bow nor be a tyrant's thrall.

St. Patrick had defied the pagan rulers
And lit the Hill of Slane with Easter fire
He traveled up and down throughout the greensward
To bring a land baptism of desire.

St. Patrick is as Irish as the shamrock
Though never was he born on Irish soil;
Today's the day the whole world would be Irish
And wear the green that makes a person royal.

The leprechauns cavort, the wee folks dancing,
The banshee's haunting cry comes on the breeze
And in the distance, ghosts of Irish heroes
Walk with their dreams beside the green-clad trees.

Lawrence Burns
Swampscott, Mass.

"HERE COMES THE PARADE!"

Evacuation Day? Saint Patrick's Day? South Boston's Day?

History marches by on the historic streets of South Boston! The ghosts of the men who manned the cannons on Dorchester Heights each March 17th march in later years with many of the same youngsters who once paraded their neighborhood streets with school bands and drum corps returned to march as war veterans. The Evacuation Day Parade, although many refer to it as the Saint Patrick's Day march, saw the great and relatively unknown politicians cheered on by countless thousands since the occasion of the first parade in 1901. South Boston salutes them, the men of Revolutionary War fame on the windswept Dorchester Heights to the sons and daughters of yesterday and today who have contributed so much to their beloved community and country.

From the tiptop of Dorchester Heights on a glorious Saint Patrick's Day, March 17th, 1776, General Washington perched his cannon in the direction of the barricaded Lord Howe in Boston Towne, and by the intensity of his glare "eyeballed" the British Lion who "blinked" and with knotted tail roared out of town. In 1847, the street circling the Heights was named in honor of Colonel John Thomas, who was in charge of fortifying the hillock.

The Hon. James A. Gallivan, Southie's legislator, secured the passage of the bill for the erection of the monument atop the Heights. Governor Walcott presented him the pen with which he had affixed his signature to the act establishing the monument. Gilbert Wait, a illustrious Southie, who, on his paternal side was descended from minutemen who fought side by side during the Revolution at Bunker Hill, Battle at Lexington and took part at Dorchester Heights, was present at the signing.

That it all occurred on Saint Patrick's Day, 1776, was ample reason for the South Boston Irish to combine the two glorious occasions into a hometown celebration. The dedication oration in 1902, by Senator Henry Cabot Lodge and other formal ceremonies were held in the assembly hall of the new South Boston High School in the shadow of the monument.

DORGAN'S

A Symbol of Happier Days

Saint Patrick, patron saint of Ireland, although familiar with pagan rites and sports, would undoubtedly recoil at the honor given him each March seventeenth. Furthermore, he would think it preposterous to have become a legendary celebrity in an American city three thousand miles away from Ireland's shores and one thousand years from being discovered. And yet, each Saint Patrick's Day in Boston, festive green bunting drapes the city streets through which countless thousands of trumpeting marchers, shamrock-spangled politicians and dewey-eyed spectators pay homage to his memory and acclaim the color of the trifoliate that served his holy purpose for the conversion of Irish pagans to the Holy Roman Catholic Church. And that he should share the unique celebration of the day with the memory of George Washington's great military victory at Dorchester Heights in South Boston on a March 17, 1776, Patrick would have found unbelievably absurd.

Dorgan's (Captain's Room), at the foot of G Street and Columbia Road, was the place to be for the Saint Patrick's Day once-a-year Irishman to be wearing both a green tie and a kiss-me-I'm Irish plastic button. The traditional corned beef and cabbage luncheon was the best, as was the whiskey. Attorney General Robert Quinn once called it all "the only authentic Irish steam bath in the country." The renown hostelry for decades past at the invitation of the incumbent Southie state senator gathered prominent political figures to exchange politically-slanted kidding as a preliminary indoor celebration to Southie's afternoon hometown parade. James Michael Curley is still remembered by Dorgan's Paddy Day habitue as the "champ orator" whose Shakespearian accentuated taffy never failed to enthrall. The local pols would always put down their beer, knives and forks to stand up and applaud when Boston's perpetual mayor came up the steep stairs to the second floor dining room that was supposed to seat 400, but on Saint Patrick's Day held nigh on to 1,000. The two favorite Republican guests at the annual shindy were former governors, Leverett Saltonstall and Frank Sargent. Neither

Dorgan's — A Symbol of Happier Days

one was to "chicken out" and returned state senator Billy Bulger's and United States Representative Joe Moakley's Irish ribbing with a quick Yankee needling. Another prime favorite was Southie's Louise Day Hicks. Always a lady, but when the need arose she could be quick with a quip or barb. And that's the way it was at Dorgan's on Paddy's Day.

March, 1973, saw the "last hurrah" of the good times at Dorgan's. The pending Boston Schools Desegregation Plan forced upon a reluctant South Boston community caused a cancellation of the yearly gathering. In a similar vein, to avoid the possibility of bitter unpleasantries to what had always been a fun occasion, the 1974 joint Evacuation Day - Saint Patrick's Day affair at Dorgan's was called off. A long-time symbol of happy times, the famous South Boston landmark was destroyed by fire on October 9, 1974.

The long tree-shaded reservation that begins its course at Columbus Park passes by the site where Irishman and Yankee roasted and toasted one another amid high revelry. The reservation is a favorite play area for Southie's sports-minded youngsters.

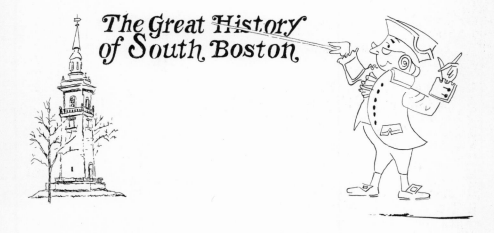

The Great History of South Boston.

South Boston's Wooden Ships and Iron Men

"SOUTH BOSTON'S WOODEN SHIPS AND IRON MEN"

1820   FREEMAN HATCH   1889

He became famous making the astonishing passage in clipper ship *Northern Light* from San Francisco to Boston in 76 days, 6 hours—an achievement won by no mortal before or since.

Pemberton writes in his *Description of Boston:* "The harbor of Boston is at this date crowded with vessels. Eighty-four sail have been counted lying at two of the wharves only. It is reckoned that not less than four hundred and fifty sail of ships, brigs, schooners, and sloops and small craft are now in port." As for the building of ships, he tells of its having been carried on at upwards of twenty-seven dockyards at one and the same time. He wrote, that in all of these yards there had been more than sixty vessels on the docks at one time. "They were nurseries and produced many hardy seamen," Pemberton vouched.

Brave ships, beautiful clippers, were still to come in seemingly endless procession. In one sense, the clippers were neither a national or racial achievement. The builders of ships came to Boston from England, Wales, Scotland, Ireland, France, Holland and the Scandinavian shores. The Yankee Clipper was a product of the "American melting pot."

Many leaders in the maritime industry came to build and to reside in South Boston, with Asa F. Baker of Baker & Morrell living at F and Broadway. Captain Fred Howes lived on Broadway near F, and the Briggs' home was not far from the shipyard at G Street.

During 1851, the famous clipper *Northern Light* was launched from the E & H Briggs' yard at the northern end of K Street on contract for the owner, James Huckins of Boston. Dimensions are (in order) tonnage: length, breadth and depth, given in feet and inches, 1021: 171.4 x 36 x 29.9.

The year 1853 was the year of clipper ship records. More important passages were made during that year than during any similar period of sailing ship history. One of the best sea derbies from San Francisco and around Cape Horn to Boston set a mark that still stands, undefeated and unequalled.

William E. Brewster, master of the clipper *Contest* (later burned by the *Alabama,* a Confederate warship) at 3:00 p.m. on Saturday, March 12, 1853, set out to sea with a following breeze bound for New York. The next afternoon, a full twenty-four hours apart, the *Northern Light,* captained by Freeman Hatch of South Boston, sailed out in pursuit.

With a spanking wind, both ships had the very unusual run of only fourteen days to the Line. On the thirty-eighth day of the race, with both clippers now off the Horn, the *Northern Light* began to gain on the *Contest,* now aft and only faintly discernible through the snow squall of the early antarctic winter. On April 23, the last encounter is thus referred to in the log of the *Contest*: April 23—Lat. 48.32 S Lon. 50.16—Comes in moderate—Latter squally with snow and rain. *Northern Light* 15 miles astern.

The two clippers did not sight each other again during the rest of the sea derby. At 6:00 p.m., May 30th, the *Contest* picked up her pilot to the Southeast of the Jersey Highlands, 80 days from San Francisco. Two days earlier the *Northern Light* had picked up her pilot at 10:00 in the evening, five miles outside of Boston Light, and Seth Doane, first officer, entered in her log: "So ends this passage of 76 days and five hours from San Francisco."

Men, like ships, never quite live out their days. Captain Freeman Hatch now dreams brave dreams on a quiet Massachusetts hillside overlooking the surges and tides of Boston Harbor. The gallant clipper ship *Northern Light* was in collision and abandoned at sea on January 2, 1861.

THE BOSTON TEA PARTY

In May, 1773, King George III of England signed a new law—The Tea Act—to regulate the sale of tea in the colonies. The act was intended to give the British East India Company the exclusive privilege of selling its tea directly to the colonists. At New York and Philadelphia the townsmen prevented the tea from being unloaded, no tax was paid and the ships sailed back to England.

At Boston, events did not proceed so smoothly. Thomas Hutchinson, the royal governor of Massachusetts, refused to permit the East India Company ships to leave Boston Harbor until the duty was paid on every tea chest in the cargo. Samuel Adams and John Hancock were leaders in the colonists' plot to dispose of the tea. At a given time, they gave the signal to a large group of local patriots gathered at the Old South Church and an inspiring event of protest began to unfold. Disguised as Mohawk Indians, about one hundred of these Sons of Liberty marched to Griffin's Wharf, dragged the tea chests (342 in number) on deck, ripped them open and dumped every leaf into Boston Harbor.

When the tea was thrown overboard, a fairly large quantity still remaining in the wooden chests floated ashore across the harbor at Mrs. Foster's farm in South Boston (now D to F Street). Mrs. Foster's hired man could not resist the temptation of collecting the tea and storing it in the farm barn. On many occasions he attempted to brew himself a pot of tea with the confiscated cargo, but Mrs. Foster would have none of it. She was a strong-minded person and a firm believer in the patriot cause. She would, on these occasions, read the riot act to her hired man and because of her stand most of the tea was never used.

The destruction of the shipment of tea was followed by the vindictive Parliamentary Bill, which closed the Port of Boston to all commercial traffic on June 1, 1774. On this day, amid "the melancholy tolling of muffled bells," Governor Hutchinson left for England.

Beaver, one of the three ships involved in the Boston Tea Party,
anchored on the Fort Point side of Boston Harbor

After reading General Gage's reports of the colonists' preparations to resist the British edicts, Parliament declared "Massachusetts to be in rebellion." Gage was ordered to use whatever force was necessary to break up the local Provincial Congress and the Minutemen organizations. In Boston, the Committee of Safety learned of General Gage's plan to arrest Adams and Hancock in Lexington. On the evening of April 19th, Paul Revere and William Dawes were selected to spread the countryside alarm that the British were beginning their march to Lexington.

Elizabeth II Docking at Commonwealth Pier, South Boston

BOSTON LOOKS TO THE FUTURE
"AHOY—LANDLUBBER!"

(Queen Elizabeth II Docking at Commonwealth Pier, Boston Harbor)

About a quarter of a million working men and women (not including an army of shoppers) come charging into Boston each week-day morning from out of buses, parking lots and underground tubes. Few rarely ponder on, or visit, Boston's many structural relics that "cradled Liberty." They seldom see the many historic wharves that border Atlantic Avenue or pause to daydream about the "clouds of sail" that for over three centuries billowed in and out of Boston Harbor with human cargo from Europe, crated tea from China and barreled rum from the Indies.

The historic wharf area, in a fashion similar to that of the now demolished Scollay Square area, with its new Government Center, has been given a new face. Sky-reaching harbor towers, a luxury residential complex on the new Boston waterfront commands an unparalleled far-out view of the harbor to where cargo ships are gathered up by escorting tugboats. The ancient red brick storehouses squatting low at the feet of the concrete giants have been converted into modern apartment quarters for the new breed of oceanside dwellers. The combined aromas of creosoted hawser, and salted fish still remain, however, to stir up visions of a memorable era.

On the South Boston shore side of the inner harbor, picturesque restaurants, along with serving the choice fruits of the ocean harvest, provide their patrons with an ever-changing panorama of the harbor with its daily sailing of vessels, transporting both native and visiting landlubbers to and around the harbor islands rich with the granite relics of a pre-Revolutionary and Civil War past.

Uncle Sam now quarters his retired battlecraft beside the great Commonwealth Pier. Strangely enough, that particular wharf area composed of the debris of the Great Boston Fire was utilized to burn up obsolete sailing vessels before the present pier was constructed.

OLD IRONSIDES

HERE WAS BUILT THE CONSTITUTION

There are other historic treasures in Charlestown besides Bunker Hill, but the Navy Yard with *Old Ironsides* beckoned the visitor first of all. As you walk her decks, ponder on the donated pennies of schoolchildren who restored the old ship. Think, too, of Oliver Wendell Holmes, whose stirring verses pleaded in preference to the planned scuttling that steamed up the efforts to preserve her. . . .

> Nail to her mast the holy flag
> Set every threadbare sail,
> And give her to the god of storms,
> The lightning and the gale!

At old Constitution Wharf in Boston's North End the great ship-yards of Edmund Hartt laid the keel of the famous battle frigate *Constitution* in November, 1794. The capabilities of Boston at that time for the construction and equipment was exemplified in the building of "Old Ironsides." The copper, bolts, and spikes, drawn from malleable copper, were furnished from Paul Revere's works. The sails were of Boston manufactured sail cloth made in the Old Granary Building. The cordage came from Boston ropewalks. The gun-carriages from a Boston shop. Only the anchors and the timber came from outside of Boston. The anchors were from the town of Hanover, twenty miles south of Boston, the oak came from Massa-chusetts and New Hampshire forests.

When the *Constitution* was first inscribed for destruction in 1830, Holmes wrote *Old Ironsides* to rouse the nation and save the ship. In 1897, Congressman John F. Fitzgerald of Boston and grandfather of President Kennedy submitted a resolution to the House of Repre-sentatives calling on the Secretary of the Navy to take steps to save it again. The ship then was reconditioned and found safe refuge in the Charlestown side of Boston Harbor.

In 1973, *Constitution* began an extensive overhauling. Senator Edward M. Kennedy of Massachusetts introduced legislation that the historically significant portions of the Boston Naval Yard at Charles-town be properly maintained and preserved and that *Ironsides* be maintained in her home port of Boston.

On August 19th, 1812, under the command of Captain Isaac Hull, the *Constitution* scored her most celebrated victory over the British frigate *Guerriere* some six hundred miles east of Boston. A Yankee gunner who saw a shot bounce off *Constitution's* oaken planking shouted: "Her sides are made of iron!" Thus she earned the name by which she is best known to millions—*Old Ironsides*.

In some sections, *Constitution's* hull was protected by more than twenty inches of frames and planking, the heaviest being near the water line. The thousands of wooden treenails to fasten timbers were immovable once swelled by ocean dampness. Her designed dimensions marked a length overall of 204 feet, with 175 feet on the low waterline; a beam of 43 feet, 6 inches; and her sailing draft was 21 feet forward and 23 feet aft. The tonnage under old measurement rules approximated 1,500 tons. Records indicate a top speed logged at thirteen and one half knots.

The "eagle of the sea" was provided with a wing spread of thirty-six sails, almost all square and made of flax. They had an area of 42,720 square feet, approximately an acre. The largest unit was the 3,440-square-foot main topsail. Well over two miles of hemp cordage were required for running rigging to manage the sails. This did not include standing rigging used to support the masts nor cordage used other places on the ship.

Although designed as a forty-four gun frigate, *Constitution* mounted fifty-five guns when she outclassed *Guerriere*. Included were thirty 24-pounders on the gun deck and twenty-two 32-pound car-ronades on the upper deck, plus two long 24-pounders and a long 18-pounder on the spar deck.

Old Ironsides was involved in the undeclared naval war with France (1798-1800), the sea battles with the Barbary Pirates (1801-1805), and the War of 1812. She fought her last battle under the command of Captain Charles Stewart, when she encountered the British frigates the *Cyane* and the *Levant* near the Madeira Islands off the African coast in February, 1815.

How many visitors to *Old Ironsides,* berthed in Boston and now the oldest warship afloat, are familiar with the incredible saga of the ship's figurehead of Andrew Jackson, which was beheaded one dark night by a young Bostonian who opposed Jackson, then President, and who presented the head to a choleric Secretary of the Navy.

I REMEMBER CASTLE ISLAND

(circa 1912)

"Doughnut Democrats," was the homely tag attached to the shirt-tails of the everyday Bostonian and his family who, of a summer afternoon, boarded the open-horse trolley to the "seaside resort" at City Point in South Boston. A five-cent fare brought as many as 70,000 on a hot summer's day to flock the three-mile long ocean resort area to share in Southie's many structural peculiarities and varied hospitalities. Loaded down with bags of doughnuts, sandwiches and beach paraphernalia, they scattered 'round and about to the many attractions of their choice.

The rambling wooden Peninsula Hotel facing Kelly's Public Landing and the neighboring Bay View Tavern, both with shaded verandas, served Uncle Mike with a huge schooner of lager beer for a nickle a glass—stronger spirits—ten cents. The third on the house. For the grand total of fifty cents, a working man could achieve a "Sunday glow" that kept him in good spirits for the entire afternoon.

Old man Hendrick's "City Point Cafe" at the corners of P and Sixth Street (later to become "Knocko's" a restaurant and bar run by the beloved Southie character and brother of the illustrious Speaker, John W. McCormick) served an excellent shore dinner to the visiting young sport and his date for fifty cents per—lager beer served only to the male sport—five cents extra. Later on the couple would "work off" the meal by strolling the "Iron Pier" leading out from the Headhouse at City Point to the tiny heart-shaped island, there to await the moon with hundreds of other young lovers, to sing and rattle the bridge's wooden planks to the sound of an Irish "cordeen" along with the colleens and their recently arrived "Dannyboy" dates.

From Kelly's Landing, the "nickle steamer" took the harbor excursionist hourly to Castle Island, a distance of slightly more than a mile. Or, the economy-minded youngster would save the five cent fare and hike the quarter-mile bridge that started off from the tip of City Point and brought him to the old granite fort, Southie's most historical and beloved picnic area.

The old fort completed in 1833, still retaining its title: Fort Independence, stands only a little different than when it was first erected. Wild shrubbery now grows from the tops of the battlements that once housed howitzers and heavy cannon. The granite casements from which guns once covered the harbor are barred with solid metal plates. The huge bolt-studded gate entrance is kept closed to keep the curious from exploring the ancient rubble behind the granite walls. The giant elm trees, storm-damaged, standing outside the Fort Gate have for two hundred years or more sheltered both venerable war heroes and visiting "doughnut democrats" while they relished their humble fare.

The old Civil War-type heavy cannon perched on top of iron carriages once used to guard the approach to Boston Harbor, were thoughtlessly appraised by government bigwigs as only scarecrows intended to add solely to the romantic charisma of the happy little island and antiquity of the old fort. In the summer of 1907, the War Department asked for bids on most of the cannon that had been perched on the upper parapets of the fort ever since the Civil War. A local junk dealer purchased the cannon and, taking the fourteen thousand pound monsters off into deep water, used dynamite to break up the guns into smaller pieces. They left six cannon on two locations close to the outer fort along with a pair of howitzers set high on the parapet directly above the so-called Fort Gate. During the Second World War, hypocritical, so-called "junk for freedom" scavengers hauled the last of the relics off to a junkyard, to the heartbreak of every kid in South Boston.

During Mayor James Michael Curley's first administration, Boston Harbor was made deeper and the approaches made wider. The ocean clay sucked up from the bottom of the channel was used as fill to construct an entire broad area adjoining Marine Park. Castle Island ceased being an island, the old wooden pile bridge was demolished and a paved road with a concrete walk took its place. The children who had been promised that the new land would be beautified as additional playground and picnic area were betrayed and the valuable land was given over to the use of private and commercial exploitation. The fenced-in area, as of 1975, is a blight and a polluting eyesore that has desecrated a historic park that was once the pride and joy of every Bostonian.

The old fort's history teems with pages of romantic intrigue, con-

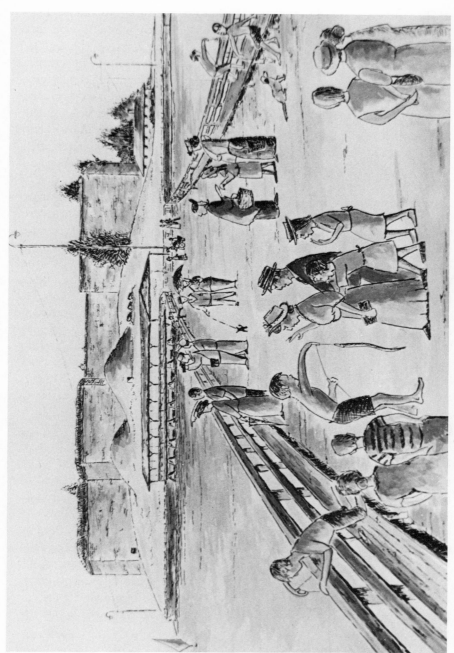

Castle Island Bridge — Fort Independence

sisting of Christmas Eve duels and subsequent secret entombment; disappointment in love resulting in suicide; rewarded romance fulfilled to the extent that 14 children were born to one resident couple; paupers, Indians, prisoners and deserters were inducted into its military as soldiers or slaves; Presidents of the United States have graced the grounds by their presence; treasure hunters have in futility dug the Island upside down amid the jeers of ghostly night-callers.

There are various blood, guts and old wives' tales of a horrific nature associated with the old fort as might be expected, relating to corpses found in out-of-the-way munition magazines, sudden and disastrous bomb explosions, and even of unexplained harbor voices loudly shouting at one another in a dreadful manner from distances of twenty miles apart: "Boy, boy come away, come away." Coming upon the old fort on a dark, bleak, windy night with the old island elms and chestnut trees shivering ghostly with sighing melancholy deep in dark shadows, one could easily believe its many spectral anecdotes. And, too, the shivering boughs could tell of ghostly figures resembling "kitchen canaries" (Irish maid servants) hastening across the wooden pile bridge leading to City Point to get back to the rectory before the pastor of St. Eulalias Church locked up for the night.

Castle Island, a 21-acre site, had its first fort built in 1634, mostly through the efforts of Governor Thomas Dudley. Dudley persuaded twenty fellow Puritans to subscribe five pounds each for the fortification of the Island and the protection of the newly found Boston Plantation. Let it be understood, now and for all times, that South Boston's contribution to American history began the day Governor Dudley and his Puritan elders rowed over to a little island in the heart of Boston Harbor and said, "We find our defense here, now let our history begin!" The group thereupon selected Deputy-Governor Roger Ludlow to take charge of the construction. Nicholas Simpkins, was given the honor of being the first commandant of the fort. Affairs in Massachusetts, however, were so peaceful that the General Court in 1642 decided the "Castle" was no longer needed and gave orders to abandon the island.

During 1645, neighboring communities helped refortify the island, agreeing on a hundred pounds for maintenance. Richard Davenport, the commanding officer, was constantly hampered by early colonial frugality. In 1654, when he asked for men and supplies, Boston contributed a "great bell" and a meagre supply of gunpowder, on the assumption, evidently, that when the powder gave out, the clanging of the bell would frighten off raiding pirates and Indian marauders. The troubles of Davenport were soon to be ended, for on a sultry night in July, 1665, while asleep on his barracks cot alongside the begrudged powder magazine, a thunderstorm came up, a bolt of lightning struck the barracks, and Davenport was killed.

The disastrous fire of March, 1673 destroyed the fort on the island. Governor Bellingham had just died and, due to the confused state of his will, the town fathers "voted" to use his money for a new fort, sixty feet square. Commander Roger Clap, who landed at Nantasket from the *Mary and John* in 1630, had fourteen children growing up at the Castle. (The "Castle" never again saw such a large multitude of kids until after the present turn of the century when as many as 10,000 boys and girls visited the beloved island on a warm summer Sunday.)

Clap's favorite son, Supply, rose to be a lieutenant under his father at the fort. When James II sent Sir Edmund Andros to be governor of New England, Clap took his large family and moved off the island, much to the relief of the colonial commissary officials. Clap resigned his job, rather than serve under the hated baronet. Later on, when the unfortunate Andros (after eight months of imprisonment on the island) was finally released, he was to leave Boston forever. When Clap died at the venerable age of 82, he was buried in the King's Chapel in Boston.

In 1691, William Stoughton became the new commander of the Castle. A distinguished preacher, he was asked to take the place of the Rev. Richard Mather when he died, but Stoughton declined. He was chief justice in the court which tried the infamous witchcraft cases, Samuel Sewall being his colleague. Stoughton reported the wretched conditions of the fort to his superiors in England, but nothing came of it until the turn of the century, when Colonel Wolfgang Romer, chief engineer of the British forces in New England, decided the old fort was beyond repair and ordered it torn down. In 1701, the actual construction of what was to be known as "Castle William" began.

In October of 1716, Lieutenant-Governor William Dummer took control at the Castle. Dummer, however, was more of an economist than a warrior. It was soon discovered that he had been regularly sending three soldiers from the fort to work on his farm at Newburg and was asking Boston to pay for their board. There was quite a political rumpus in the colonial legislature, which believed the circumstances were most unusual, even though Dummer's accounts were finally accepted.

A committee of inspection in 1736 found everything at the Castle in good condition. A new battery was erected at a fifty-yard distance from the fort. Moreover, in 1750, new barracks three hundred and sixty feet long were erected for the soldiers of William Pepperell, the hero of Louisburg, who became commander of Castle William in 1757.

In 1761, Governor Francis Bernard, blamed for most of the pre-revolutionary trouble in Boston, was sorely confused in deciding his problems. With the passage of the Stamp Act in 1765, however, he was sharp enough to have controversial stamps hidden at the Castle. Vigorous Boston opposition caused the return of the stamps to England.

In the struggle between England and the Colonies, Boston was considered to be the center of attack and resistance, and Castle William "a key to be grasped by the strongest hand." When Bernard sailed out of Boston Harbor in 1769, a short period of calm prevailed. Lieutenant-Governor Hutchinson was now in command of the Island. The fort was badly in need of repairs, and the equivalent of fifty thousand dollars was expended to bring the Castle up to snuff. Colonel Montresor of His Majesty's Engineers put the two hundred guns on the island in prime condition, but the cagey Bostonians were reluctant to help the project, fearing that the guns could at sometime in the future be turned against them—as turned out to be the case.

On the second day of March, 1770, a dispute between British soldiers and a Boston citizen started up a fracas (The Boston Massacre), wherein three citizens were killed and five others wounded. The 14th and 20th regiments were forced to leave Boston and, as a result of the massacre, were ordered to the Castle to avoid further confrontations. Many prominent Bostonians, loyal to the English King, in danger to their lives fled to the Castle for protection. Most passed a hard and cruel New England winter in the damp and bitter-cold casemates.

Although it is claimed that the Castle never participated in actual warfare, it was indeed under fire in the month of March, 1776. On the fifth of the month, Lord Percy, under orders from General Howe, proceeded to attack the Americans belligerently scowling down on the beleagured British troops from atop Dorchester Heights. The Castle cannon directed a withering fire against the various American gun emplacements on the mainland, (City Point) but the Continentals answered shot for shot. Whereupon, Percy embarked with his regiments from the castle for an assault on Washington on the Heights. A terrible New England gale suddenly arose and drove the British longboats in the opposite course, clear over to Governor's Island on the Noodles Island side of the Harbor.

Thoughtfully then—if Percy's transports had successfully combatted the storm and Howe's troops driving through the Roxbury Neck had mutually joined in the planned attack, one ponders the result. Successful, it would have smothered Washington's plans in slaughter, final defeat and put the Virginian in King George's hunting bag. Unsuccessful, it would have meant the extermination of Howe's army and his recall to England. This engagement was the only battle in which the fort ever participated. Strangely enough, the guns on the fort were directed against the very people they were meant to protect.

With the Continentals firmly entrenched at Dorchester Heights, the British knew they would leave Boston. On March 20, as they were passing out of the Harbor, they stopped at the fort and left the Castle ablaze and, as a final gesture of contempt, blew up Boston Light. General Washington sent Paul Revere and a company of men to repair the damage to the fort. Revere's fame rests largely on his "midnight ride" to warn the farmers of Lexington and Concord that the "redcoats" were on their way. Paul abandoned his horse to participate in naval exploits. He served an expedition to Rhode Island, but then never saw action again.

Richard Gridley, the hero of Louisburg, supervised the erection of a rebuilt fortress in 1778, and added guns to the defense taken from the wrecked British frigate *Somerset*. John Hancock assumed control of the castle in 1779. Hancock relinquished his command to Lieutenant-Governor Cushing in 1781. Under Cushing, John Howard's famous prison reform system was tried in Massachusetts with Castle Island as its location. A small group of convicts was sent from the mainland to what was to be the first state prison in Massachusetts. They were not the first prisoners at the Castle, for in earlier days Indian prisoners had been forced to help build or rebuild the fort. King Philip, sachem of the Wampanoags, complained of it.

Governor Hancock again resumed charge of the Castle until 1793, when Samuel Adams assumed the leadership until 1797, whereupon Governor Sumner took command. Massachusetts offered the cession of the Castle to the National Government and, on the second of October, 1798, Major Daniel Jackson formally accepted Castle William on behalf of the United States of America. President John Adams participated in the ceremony held in August, 1799, at the changing of the name to Fort Independence.

During the short war with France, prisoners were landed at the fort. At one time, 248 Frenchmen were contained in the prison. There is no doubt that conditions for the imprisoned on the island were both severe and unhealthy. Closely confined in cold, damp dungeons and fed poorly, it can be presumed that illnesses and death took their toll. Excavations on the island have in several incidents unearthed the evidence. It is conceivable that "good Indians" and Frenchmen never left the Island. (A "good Indian" was then considered "a dead one".)

The work of rebuilding Fort Independence started May 7, 1801. Lieutenant-Colonel Tousard was the constructing engineer. When the fort was completed, Nehemiah Freeman, the commander, named each of the five bastions. He called the east bastion, "Winthrop"; the southern "Shirley"; the north, "Dearborn"; the northeast, "Adams"; and the western bastion, "Hancock."

The old fort has a romantic and an eerie past. The most whimsically strange tale narrates the Massie duel. During a card game on Christmas Eve, 1817, a young Virginian, Robert Massie was accused of cheating and challenged an older officer to a duel. After their mutual friends tried hard to negotiate sense, the duel began. Massie, fatally stabbed, died that Christmas afternoon. In May of 1827, a young man, Edgar A. Perry enlisted and was stationed at the fort. His real name was Edgar Allen Poe. His curiosity aroused by the monument on the island erected to the slain duelist's memory, he inquired as to what had become of the victor of the tragedy. The story related to Poe became one of the most macabre ever to be recorded in the fort's history. A group of Massie's friends, seeking revenge, got the victor drunk and carried him deep down into a small dungeon underneath the fort. Chaining him to the floor, they bricked up the entrance and deserted him. The complete story was recorded in Edgar Allen Poe's "The Cask of Amontillado."

It happened that in 1905, when workmen were repairing the base of the fort, they came upon a blank wall that, according to the plans, should have been a small cell. Breaking through the wall, they came upon a skeleton with the remains of an 1812 army uniform still hanging on it. The officer's remains were removed and given a decent burial. Massie's remains and his memorial was moved from the island in 1892, across the Harbor to Governor's Island. The relics were removed again to Resthaven Cemetery on Deer Island in 1908 and once again to Fort Devens in 1939.

Henry Lawrence Eustis was born at Castle Island in 1819. The son of General Abraham Eustis, Henry attended Harvard College, graduating with the class of 1838. He also followed the military tradition by attending West Point, where he was a classmate of Ulysses S. Grant. In 1843, he was in charge of military construction at Lovell's and George's Islands in Boston Harbor, leaving to join the faculty of Harvard. When the Civil War bugles sounded in 1861, he left the college to become a colonel in the Tenth Massachusetts Infantry.

At the start of the war, Major-General Arnold, in command at Fort Independence, reported very few serviceable guns at the fort. Although Governor Andrew tried to obtain cannon from England, many months passed before Boston was adequately fortified. The Fourth Massachusetts Battalion was quartered at the fort, and among its honored men were Charles Francis Adams and William Francis Bartlett. Bartlett left the Junior Class at Harvard in 1861, trained at the island and was given a captain's commission in the twentieth Regiment. A month later in the thick of the war, a bullet shattered his left knee so badly that the leg had to be amputated. Sent north, Bartlett returned to battle less than a year later. Because of the loss of his leg, the gallant soldier rode into battle on horseback. The only mounted officer, he was an easy target for the rifle of a Southern rebel. Recovering again from his wound, he rejoined the army in time to be captured at Petersburg. He never fully recovered from sickness contracted in prison. The year 1876, brought an end to his honorable career. He was the most conspicuous soldier New England sent to the Civil War.

In the year 1879, Fort Independence was closed up as an active

commissioned defense in order that the garrisons might be concen-
trated at Fort Warren, and Ordinance-Sergeant Maguire was left in
charge of the island.   In 1888, the City of Boston made tentative
plans to place the island in the hands of the Park Department.
Congressman Collins from South Boston passed a resolution through
the legislature allowing the city to extend a causeway around the
island, but President Grover Cleveland vetoed the idea, stating that
"the resolution under consideration should not, for reasons stated,
become 'operative'."   Three years later however, because of continuing pressure by concerned Bostonians, the Government reversed its
decision and a bridge, paid for by Boston taxpayers, was built that
reached Castle Island from Marine Park at City Point.

When the Spanish War broke out in 1898, Uncle Sam took the fort
away from Boston and converted the Island into a mine and torpedo
station.   While there were many war scares involving Boston and the
Spanish Fleet, neither guns nor mines were discharged in defense of
Boston.   When the Spanish-American War was over, Castle Island was
returned to the people of Boston.

Castle Island continues to make history in a homely modern
fashion.   Daily, of a bright summer's day, thousands of hikers,
motorists and their gathered families cross over the causeway to the
island—there to picnic in the shadow of the fort, broil hamburgers
under the giant elms, swim Pleasure Bay, or fish from off the island's
docks.   But it is here where, if one obtains permission to enter the
forbidden interior of the ancient fortress, Boston's early history
can, at the beckoning of the romantic and imaginative, be resurrected.

Once again, within the high granite walls, Colonial governors
converse.   Barked orders to ancient regimental units resound.   The
dusty, deserted barracks re-echoes with the cadenced shuffle of feet
alerted by the chanticleer blare of bugles summoning the blue clad
Civil War cadets to their sparse rations.   The enormous brick ovens
in smoke-stained chambers still retain the soot and ashes of ten
thousand baking fires—aye—even the ghostly smell of yesteryears'
crusty army bread captures a lively imagination.   Dim light entering
through the many wall-lined, narrow gun apertures, halos each and
every chamber.   Here in the northern bastion, war prisoners scrawled
names and left the stains of their anguish on white-washed dungeon
walls or carved on a bolt-studded oaken door.

"I Remember Castle Island"

Here too, and once again, the chambers re-echoes the wail of a newborn babe or the happy chattering of children amid the drone of school lessons being taught. Or the raucous talk of ghostly soldiers gathered in the mess hall finds cadence with the sound of tin cups and plates being shuffled around on wooden tables. Each bastion has a veritable history all its own, and the scars of decades speak in retrospect.

The stone steps on the far west side of the inner fort lead 40 feet upward to the parapet that, according to a drawing made in 1850, had 36 heavy cannon. Earth and debris cover the emplacements where guns once hung their muzzles over the edges of the ramparts. Each of the five bastions have ammunition depots reaching deep down into the bowels of the fort, and here again, inches thick with debris and soil washed down into the passages these many years past. The only living creatures tolerated on the parapets to heed the ghosts of artillerymen are the rats that scurry the dark, dank passages, and the birds that twitter from off the treetops growing tall from the soil covering the bastions.

Demolition laid claim in 1969 to the lone remaining residence on the Island. Once the fort commandant's quarters, it stood a hundred feet from the Fort Gate; had a large cellar containing dungeons used for VIP prisoners when the island fort was activated. A romantic event took place here on August 12, 1919, when Lieut. Albert Hegenberger married Louise Lindberg the resident daughter of the Lindberg family. Hegenberger, completed the first non-stop flight from the U. S. to Hawaii in 1927. Previous to the demolition, the white painted residence had a well-kept garden and several fruit and lilac bushes growing on the wire-enclosed premises.

Old traditions and new projects converged at the State House on Beacon Hill and at the old fort on Castle Island on a bleak late afternoon in October, 1971. The Flag Heritage Foundation had completed work for the new official state flag, maritime flag, and Governor's flag of Massachusetts.

Flag Heritage Day derives its name from the fact that it was 185 years to the day that Governor James Bowdoin presented a flag to the First Corps of Cadets. An exact replica was presented to Governor Sargent by a Color Guard dressed in authentic 1786 First Corps of Cadets uniforms. That same afternoon the Flag Heritage Foundation and the Veterans Association of the First Corps of Cadets hosted ceremonies at the fort where another replica of the 1781 Fort Independence flag was hoisted. The original flag is too fragile to be used in public and is kept behind glass in the State House.

The Massachusetts National Guard provided a display of 21 historic banners for the ceremonies at the fort. The flags were carried by local high school girls, and a Massachusetts Battery, a reactivated Civil War unit, performed drill to appropriate fife and drum music in the pageantry that followed.

At the ceremony, the officials of the Metropolitan District Commission urged community cooperation to aid in securing legislative appropriation to be used for extensive renovation and repair of the historic Castle in the hope that it "will again become a show place within two years and certainly on the bicentennial of the War for Independence."

Thompson's Island — Dorchester Bay

THOMPSON'S ISLAND

(circa 1884)

"'And here at pleasure may you happy live
For here with joy and dutiful regard
In all rural comforts. . .shared.'"

Nathaniel Hawthorne in "Passages" from the *American Notebooks* (Boston, 1884) writes. . ."An excursion aboard a steamboat to visit the Manual Labor School for Boys. . .Examination and exhibition of the boy, little tanned agriculturists. . .examining the products, as wheat in sheaves on the stubblefield. Oats, great pumpkins elsewhere; pastures; mowing ground. All cultivated by the boys. Their residence, a great brick building, painted green, and standing on the summit of a raising ground."

Few schools have had a more distinguished roster of founders than Thompson's Academy. They were men of promise and influence in the Boston scene that brought into sharp focus the need for proper care and education of boys in distressed Boston families; boys who were the victims of conditions, both economic and social, for which they were in no way responsible and unable to combat.

At a meeting of the Society, held on the 5th of November, 1832, it was reported that a suitable farm had been purchased in Boston Harbor for $6,000 and that the Reverend Eleaser M. P. Wells had been engaged as Superintendent. It was Mr. Wells who chose the site for the wharf and future buildings and with two assistants and fourteen boys moved to the Island and took up residence. During the first summer, they broke ground for the Main Building which the boys helped build. They also built a cook house for the workmen, a bridge over a ditch and a barn. They dug a well and cleaned the spring. The livestock at the time consisted of oxen, cows and sheep. When the crops were harvested they were stored in the new barn. In October, the front and back projections and the southeast wing of the main building were completed and the rest of the boys moved to the Island.

The Farm School's growing family of boys farmed in season on fair days and studied and worked indoors when it was rainy. In the evening, during the winter months, the boys were taught the first principles of husbandry and horticulture. Their moral and religious

Pilgrim II – Iron Pier – Stone Heart

education was well cared for and habits of orderliness and industry established. Thus, the general pattern was set for the operation of the Farm School, which was carried on for many years.

Thompson's Academy "Farm and Trade School Band" is shown being ferried by the steamer *Pilgrim II* from Thompson's Island across Dorchester Bay to Kelly's Landing at City Point in South Boston.

Today, when one views Thompson's Island, it is difficult to believe that it once was covered by an ice-sheet almost a mile thick. The great mass of ice extended some fifty miles out in the Atlantic Ocean and, because of its great weight, the land was depressed as much as four hundred feet. The ice-mass eventually removed, the land beneath it rose gradually, the higher portions becoming islands and mainlands in others.

The recorded history of the Island may be traced back to the year 1621, when a shallop made its way slowly up the coast from the Plimoth Plantation. Aboard the craft were Captain Miles Standish, nine Englishmen and three Indians, one of whom was Squanto that colorful figure of early new England history. Captain Standish and a sailor explored the Island, taking possession for David Thompson. From 1621 to 1832, there were twenty-four individuals who, at one time or another, owned Thompson's Island. In 1832, it was bought for use as a Farm School and the Island was annexed to the city of Boston. Thompson's Academy is the fifth oldest preparatory school for boys in New England in continuous operation, which with independent funds provided the public service.

The "Band" that began its illustrious inception in 1857, finally gave way to more urgently needed scholastic directives. According to Thompson's Academy historian Raymond W. Stanley, some 12 boys were casually amusing themselves one afternoon by creating musical sounds through combs covered with tissue paper. They were soon joined by three boys with violins, and this group of 15 began to schedule informal meetings on a regular basis. In the *Four Thompsons,* Stanley writes: "A bass violin, saxhorn, cornopean, and a drum were added to form the nucleus of what became, that same year, the first school band in America." Thompson's Academy can reflect with pride upon the fact that 12 of their early brethren are responsible for the school band concept which, during the last 115 years, has developed into an integral part of school life throughout much of the world.

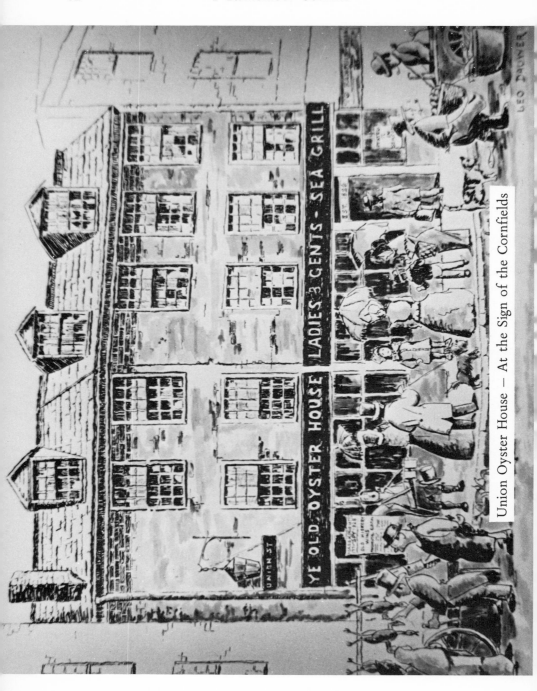

Union Oyster House — At the Sign of the Cornfields

AT THE SIGN OF THE CORNFIELDS
(circa 1826)
Union Oyster House, Union Street, Boston

Your visit to Boston would not be complete without a dinner at the Olde Union Oyster House on Union Street in Boston's famous North End, which has been doing business since 1826, with the same stalls and oyster bar in their original positions.

On the second floor of this building lived Louis Philippe, afterwards King of France. Here, during his exile, he taught the French language to many prominent Bostonians of the period.

Previous to 1826, it had been the well-known store of Thomas Capen, importer of silks and fancy dress goods, and was known as "At the sign of the Cornfields." Thomas Capen succeeded his father, Hopestill Capen, with whom in 1769, Benjamin Thompson of Woburn, afterwards Count Rumford, was apprenticed as clerk.

In the upper part of the building, patriot printer Isaiah Thomas from 1771 to the beginning of hostilities of the Revolutionary War in April 1775, published the *Massachusetts Spy* that helped inspire unity among the colonies. Hounded by the British authorities, his life threatened, Thomas, in the still of the night of April 16, 1775, rowed his press over to Charlestown and put it on an ox-cart. Enroute to Worcester, the printer was at the opening of hostilities on Lexington Green and at the "Old North Bridge" in Concord.

During a part of the Revolutionary War period, Ebenezer Hancock, a paymaster of the Continental Army, had his headquarters in the building.

In 1972, the Oyster House annexed the newly designed "1826 Room" to the ancient dining rooms on the second floor of the establishment. Newly refurbished, the "1826 Room" is reminiscent of the Jacksonian period of American history.

The old Capen House appears today much as it was when the first mayors of Boston were served their favorite oyster stew which, naturally, has been a favorite of the house ever since.

(Oyster Bar, Union Oyster House, Union Street, Boston, Mass.)

The Colonial U-shaped mahogany oyster bar is where Daniel Webster was a constant customer. "He drank a tall tumbler of brandy and water with each half dozen of oysters and seldom had less than six plates."

The oyster bar today looks out and across to the new Boston Government Center area, that was once the heart of old Scollay Square. In 1826, Hawes Atwood opened Ye Olde Oyster House. The same stalls—the same oyster bar that Mr. Atwood installed—are in their original positions today.

Hawes Atwood sold oysters wholesale—and purveyed seafood for some 66 years. In 1893, Mr. Atwood employed Allen Bacon. He soon retired and left Mr. Bacon to carry on the business—and to eventually employ Fred Greaves. Since Mr. Greaves bought the business in 1912, the Union Oyster House has known only three proprietors in its 111 years. Fred Greaves willed the property to his brother Laurence Greaves whose son Richard Greaves is presently both manager and treasurer of the establishment. Thus, the Oyster House in its entire 146 years has been in the control of three families.

In the last century the notables of Boston were familiar sights in old Union Street and behind the small-paned windows of the oyster bar, they ranged their beaver hats on the wall pegs. Their long sparrow-fashioned coat-tails hung down from bar stools and, with noses tilted upward, they slurped down heaps of tobasco-dipped raw oysters. The white-coated experts who deftly made edible the oysters on banner days hulled as many as thirty-five barrels of Cape Cod's finest and most succulent Cotuits.

Time and devoted usage will add its illustrious patina to the ancient establishment and nostalgia to its flavor.

BOSTON CITY HOSPITAL

(circa 1915)

"A Time of Change" — *James Michael Curley*

"If you didn't have the money to buy health care in the private sector, then the City Hospital was the place to go."

They said of James Michael Curley, four times mayor of Boston that "he was a legend in his own lifetime." Among today's king-makers, there are those that claim Curley's incarnation as a haloed humanitarian began during his first term in office when he evinced an extraordinary interest in Boston City Hospital.

As a lad, Curley was reared in the dispirited hospital environment of Northampton Street and often witnessed the horse-drawn ambulance or paddy wagon with their hourly cargo of misfortunates. The sight of the dying, the neglected old, the injured workman, or the unfortunate in the last stages of galloping consumption made a strong impression on the boy's mind.

During his first administration he had medical stations built or reserviced. The Boston City Hospital had additional buildings erected, or ells added. Capable doctors, nurses and key personnel of the highest order were continuously employed by the hundreds to make the hospital the best serviced and the most envied in New England.

And yet, it was his one-time detractors that most honestly recognized his labors. *The Boston Herald* that had not always "seen eye to eye" with Curley acknowledged his beneficence to the unfortunate. . ."The Passing of a Prodigy". . .a job with the City or a contractor for the father laid off at the plant. A bed and care at the City Hospital for the exhausted mother. . .unless you have been poor and forlorn in a big city, you have no conception of what this means.

Death was no stranger to Curley, it had visited him tragically all too often. Perhaps one could rationalize that this was the reason for

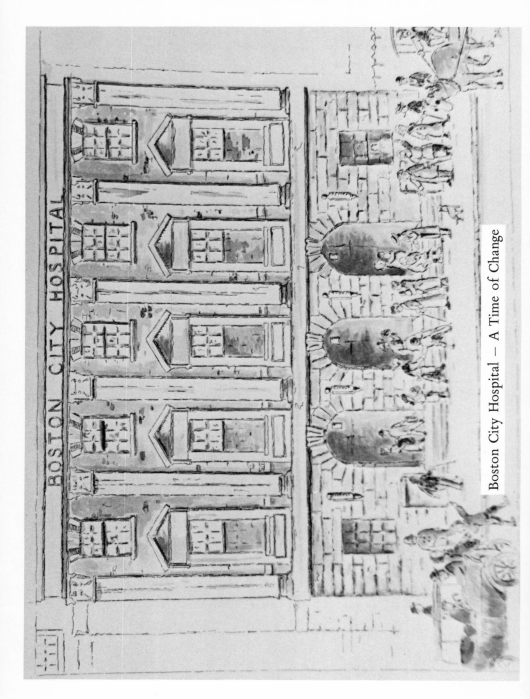

Boston City Hospital – A Time of Change

his moments of compassionate generosity, whether to those he loved, or to a total stranger who held out a hand in appeal. James Michael Curley died on November 12, 1959, eight days before reaching his eighty-fourth birthday.

THE HONORABLE JAMES MICHAEL CURLEY

(50 Years in Politics)

1900-1901	Boston Common Council
1902-1903	Representative (State Legislature)
1904-1909	Alderman
1910-1911	City Council
1911-1914	Congressman
1914-1918	Mayor
1917	Defeated for Mayor by J. J. Peters
1922-1926	Mayor
1924	Defeated for Governor by Alvin T. Fuller
1930-1934	Mayor
1935-1936	Governor
1936	Defeated for U. S. Senator by Henry Cabot Lodge, Jr.
1937	Defeated for Mayor by Maurice J. Tobin
1938	Defeated for Governor by Leverett Saltonstall
1940	Defeated for Mayor by Maurice J. Tobin
1943	Congressman
1945	Mayor

The Name Is the Old City Hall

1865   # THE OLD CITY HALL   1972

(The name is the "Old City Hall")

The address is 41-45 School Street, Boston, Mass. Its architecture is French Provincial, has six floors, and as of 1975 was 110 years old. The main entrance faces the School Street door of the Parker House and the left wing borders the rear of King's Chapel on Tremont Street.

In 1971, when the U. S. Interior Department designated 38 buildings as national historic landmarks, 19 were in Massachusetts. Important among them as architectural landmarks was Boston's Old City Hall, reflecting the eclectic taste of mid-nineteenth century America.

In January, 1969 the Press Corps vacated the premises for the New City Hall located in the New Government Center. Before they left, Bob Aldrich of the *Record American* wrote a poem telling of the newsmens' devotion for the old building.

> "Ye who pass, pause and pray
> For the generations of scribes who went this way
> For 104 years we suffered the idiosyncrasies
> Of politicians,
> Of editors,
> Of bartenders,
> Of peddlers and creditors,
> And of women beset with moral delinquencies,
> Pray for us, today for us.
> Ye, who pass, pause and pray.
> We've gone to Hell.
> We've gone away!"

The New City Hall — Classic Yankee

THE NEW BOSTON CITY HALL

(circa 1972)

"Classic Yankee"

Boston's New City Hall, finished in 1968, takes a thoughtful recognition of Faneuil Hall, Dock Square and Quincy Market, yet is a controversial and powerful architectural evolution in its own right. The design was chosen after the first national competition for a municipal building since San Francisco's city hall in 1909. The shape of New City Hall, however, like all classic Yankee architecture, is closely related to the physical embodiments of a life and land style.

The jump between Old City Hall (architects, Gridley, Bryant and Gilman) and New City Hall (architects Kallman, McKinnell and Knowles) signifies the leap from a traditionalism once the dominating factor of Massachusetts architecture, to the threshold of the twenty-first century.

The New Boston City Hall is centered in the area of the North End of Boston, formerly the Scollay Square section and the renowned tenderloin of Boston. Today, the many structures comprising the government center stand like silent Goliathian gravestones to mark the passing of the happy hunting ground whose bourgeois visitors, once seeking varied entertainment, have long since fled or ceased to be. The New Government Center, of which the City Hall is a predominant sepulcher-like structure, is a burial ground which the ghosts of its former inhabitants would be abashed to haunt.

Kevin White, first Boston Mayor to take abode in the lofty structure, twice defeated South Boston's Louise Day Hicks for the honor of being the castle's first tenant.

Park Street Church and State House

"BRIMSTONE CORNER"

(circa 1965)
Park Street Church and State House
on the edge of the Boston Common

My Country 'tis of thee
Sweet land of liberty
Of thee we sing—

One century and a quarter ago our national hymn "America" was born. Written by Samuel Francis Smith, a Baptist clergyman, it was first publicly sung in Boston at a Fourth of July celebration in 1832. It was sung that same year by Sunday School children of the Park Street Church in front of the Old Massachusetts State House.

The "perfectly felicitous Park Street Church," as Henry James calls it—admired for the beauty of its site as the focal center of rich city vistas, and its "values" as an architectural monument: the grace of its composition, its crowning feature of tower and tall, slender, graceful steeple from whence time was tolled—dates from 1809-1810. It was erected for the church founded in 1808 to revive Trinitarianism. The old Calvinism was preached here with such fervor that local wits affectionately called the angle it faces "Brimstone Corner."

The Burial Ground, the "Granary," edging the church on the Tremont Street side takes its name from a former storehouse of grain that once occupied the site of the Park Street Church. There the parents of Benjamin Franklin, its filial inscription, were laid to rest. There, too, are three signers of the Declaration of Independence, with James Otis, Samuel Adams, and Paul Revere—all of Revolutionary War measure. Here entombed also, are the one black (Crispus Attucks) and four white victims of the "Boston Massacre."

In the new Massachusetts State House, Charles Bulfinch, our first professional architect, gave Bostonians and the world a basic idea of what a state house ought to be—sweeping pillared facade, substantial dome, cupola. The dome, sheathed in copper by Paul Revere, was painted gray; since 1874 it has been covered with gold leaf. The tangible sacred cod hangs here in unbroken succession to the one in the Old State House until 1797. It established the colony and fed it and prospered great fortunes, fattening to this day.

The sacred cod, symbol of the Commonwealth's first source of wealth, is 4 ft. 11½ in. long and has been hanging in the Massachusetts State House since 1784. The carving was the idea of John Rowe (of Boston Tea Party fame) and presumedly carved out of good Massachusetts pine by John Welch.

The cod provided the early Boston Puritans with food and fertilizer for the maize the Indians taught them to cultivate. The pounds and pence derived from the barter of cod to the West Indies in exchange for molasses, tobacco and rum started up the Massachusetts ship-building industry which, in turn, nurtured the first Boston fortunes in the middle of the eighteenth century.

THE BUSIEST CORNER ON BOSTON'S BUSIEST STREET

(circa 1910)

Washington Street at the Height of the Shopping Hour

The South Boston Railroad, one of the first major builders of the primitive horsecar began converting to the electric type trolley car during and shortly after the "Gay Nineties." The Boston Elevated Railway, having consolidated Metropolitan Boston's surface and subway surface lines, continued the use of the summertime open 9-bench electrics (some of the oldest were reconditioned horsecars dating back to the Civil War era) and the summer of 1919 was their last season. Management increased its roster of electric semi-convertables, (closed cars) which could be operated year round. When vehicular traffic on Boston's scheduled trolley lines increased, the electrics finally gave way to the more off-track and maneuverable bus service.

The three main passenger service lines upon which today's modern buses traverse from the South Boston Peninsula destrict to Boston Proper (where transfers at various points throughout the Metropolitan Boston areas can be made) are basically the same routes that the primitive horsecar and trolley once traversed.

1. The *Bay View* trolley operated from Marine Park at City Point (North Point Carhouse), ran East Sixth Street to K Street, continued East Eighth to Andrew Square, thence to Dudley Street Terminal in Roxbury. Transfers available on overhead electrics. To return via the same route.

2. From City Point the *Summer Street Extension* traversed East Fourth Street to L Street, continued along Summer Street to the South Station and thence to Washington Street's shopping district. Returning via Broadway Extension, it traversed the entire length of Broadway to L Street. From L Street it went to East Fourth, then returned to the carhouse.

3. The *North Station* trolley ran from City Point, Fourth to L

The Busiest Corner on Boston's Busiest Street

Street. It covered all of Broadway to Broadway Extension. Subway cars were available east to Dorchester—west to Cambridge. Crossing Broadway Bridge the trolley went to Lower Broadway to continue via the subway for various transfers available at Park Street Under. Leaving Park Street Under to Scollay Square, it concluded the run at the North Station.

South Bostonians, since the Civil War era, wholeheartedly shared in progressing Dame Bostonia's historic business life. The men folk found jobs in the foundries, factories and the business offices. Thousands served as policemen, firemen, truckers and in Boston government. Women folk found employment in the offices, banks and in the retail establishments. Local youngbloods trolleyed their dates to the Washington Street and Scollay Square funtime centers. Afterwards, they went to dine at nearby Chinatown or at the many famous North End restaurants.

Perhaps the most enthusiastic of yesteryear's trolley passengers were Boston's grandmas, who thronged and shopped Filene's Basement, renowned throughout New England; Gilchrist's "The Friendly Store," whose great Sales Manager sales events were the "talk of the town," Jordan Marsh's basement "Dollar Day" and Raymond's "Where-U-Bot-The-Hat" taxed the trolley cars with passengers and bundles alike.

Perhaps, too, the paging of the names of these fine old department stores((many still in business) will bring an awakening nod from Boston's senior citizens. Jordan's (Jordan Marsh), Gilchrist's, Filene's, Shuman's, Raymond's, Bacon's, Segal's, Shepherd's, Chandler's, Stearn's, White's, Hollander's, Hovey's, Houghton & Dutton, Leopold Morse, Kennedy's, Vorenberg's, —and, of course, the Jeweler's Building on Washington Street, of which great grandpa sings—"When That Old Wedding Ring Was New."

Selling anything from thimbles to motorcars "Gilchrists, The Friendly Store" during the 1920's placed the Essex (the latest in touring cars) in its large Washington Street display window. Gilchrist fits easily into planning a bicentennial historical celebration. The first department store in Boston, the first store with a suburban branch and the first to hire a female salesperson, the family store takes pride in their innovative past. Gilchrist. . .a whole new place, looks ahead to a bright new future.

Boston Common's Common People

BOSTON COMMON'S COMMON PEOPLE

(circa 1973)

"God must love the common people, because He made so many of them."

Abe Lincoln

Bearded, ungainly, dour in facial expression, politically ridiculed at times beyond human endurance, President Lincoln the Great Emancipator, reincarnated, would find congenial surroundings and a heedful ear among the Boston Common's common people in forwarding his militant cause in behalf of the Blacks.

From out her Beacon Street window facing the Common, Julia Ward Howe—if she, too, came alive, would once again, thrill to the echoing verses of her inspired *Battle Hymn of the Republic* mingled with the accordion squeezin's and the drum-thumpin' of the Common's one-man band.

The Boston Park Department provided the Common's devotees with a huge graffito whitewashed sounding board (Let Each Man His Own Censor Be) whereon they scribbled happy worded memorabilia (Mamie La Tour is back in town) or passed harsh judgment on the political, social or economic problems of the time.

By informative pamphlet, strident soapbox oratory, or cajoling hymns the workaday pedestrians are urged by the Common's crusaders to return to Jesus, vote a dark horse candidate or buy a bag of peanuts to feed the Common's common pigeons. Balloons sent aloft by a crippled "Reverend" with an African Pygmy parrot perched on top of his head voices the skyborn message that "Jesus Saves."

Sun-loving old people—the so-called "Golden Age" group, sitting singly on the brick street planters lining the Tremont Street Mall seek out for a friendly face and ear in the hope that a moment can be spared them wherein a heart's nostalgic reservoir can spill out gallant dreams that used to be—or never were.

The Common's common people dream brave dreams. Though this corner of the Common is one of Boston's busiest, and seemingly indifferent to its 350 historic years, it is still the stretch where dreams are born and "Untaught Dreamers" walk with history.

Traffic Problem — Scollay Square — "Those Were the Days"

TRAFFIC PROBLEM—SCOLLAY SQUARE

(circa 1912)

"Those Were The Days"

Scollay Square was named for William Scollay, a frugal Scotsman who once owned a building there. To locate the local where Scollay Square's visiting humanity once teemed, a sightseer must follow the Freedom Trail's little red footprints beginning at Boston Common's Brimstone Corner at the old Park Street Church; pass the Parker House on Tremont Street some one hundred yards to come upon the burial ground where the ghosts of the demolished tenderloin would today be abashed to haunt.

Boston's new Government Center with its many window-sprinkled monuments stand like huge gravestones to mark the passing of Scollay Square that up to the late 50's lured the unwary. High among the many attractions that captivated Boston's Brahmin, bourgeois, unwary sightseers, adventuresome youth, visiting seamen and "women beset with moral delinquencies" were the many theatres that predominated the "Square." There was the Scollay Square, Rialto, Palace, Star and the Beacon, all of which featured smalltime vaudeville and the movies. The Old Howard on Howard Street and Waldron's Casino on Hanover Street featured traveling burlesque shows. All the great "burlycue strippers" of the era appeared here, as did Boston Irish John L. Sullivan, World's Heavyweight Boxing Champion and other sports and stage celebrities. Joe & Nemo's hot dog emporium (across the alley from where the Old Howard enticed) nourished the "two-bit sport." Two hot dogs, apple pie, coffee—25 cents.

For a dollar bill, the youthful adventurer could see Mamie La Tour belly-button tantalize, eat at Joe & Nemo's, visit a tattoo parlor, shoot a game of kelly pool, win a kewpee doll at the shooting gallery and still have a nickle left for carfare back home.

The Old Howard — "Always Something Doing!"

THE OLD HOWARD—"ALWAYS SOMETHING DOING"

(circa 1919)

In 1845, the magnificent newly-built Howard Athenaeum in Gothic design with three huge ecclesiastical windows designed by Isaiah Rogers rapidly gained fame as the most noteworthy of Boston's theatres. The first time grand opera was sung in Italian in the United States was in this solid granite structure. Jewels and silk-flossy gowns sparkled and glowed against a masculine penguin-garbed background in the gilded balconies where Boston's best bred blue-bloods applauded wildly the Italian sung arias even though none of them understood a word of Italian.

In 1961, the wrecker's ball bashed its way through a leveled Scollay Square, right up to the scorched ruins of the Old Howard, beloved bastion of the ages—and of all ages. Beneath the sign: "THE OLD HOWARD, ALWAYS SOMETHING DOING — 1 TO 11 P. M." passed furtive, school-hooking youth, eager for post-puberty adventure or legions of the aging, bald and fat recall moments that used to be or never were. But what went on at the Old Howard was honest sex—almost innocent and naive against today's pornographic skin-flicks or the shows put on by Combat Zone strippers.

Among the comic talents for whom the Howard was a "training school in burlesque" were Phil Silvers, Bert Lahr, Bud Abbott and Lou Costello. Talents closely observed—"bumps and grinds"—by Harvard boys whose education was not considered complete by the upper classmen until the freshmen had seen Ann Corio.

Ann Corio fondly recalls that "the Harvard Class of 1937 elected me to its membership and at the 25th reunion in 1962, my picture was in the special anniversary yearbook with everyone elses."

There was an ancient legend that all burlesque strippers were good-hearted and that shouts of "take it off" mingled with the exhilerating beat of a beer barrel polka never went unanswered. Gypsy Rose

Lee, Ann Corio, Peaches, Rose La Rose, Winnie Garret, Hinda Wassau—phantom lovelies, strong husky girls—all generously proportioned and with impish grins, twisted and torso-popped the entire length of the stage until only a g-string dangled provocatively.

After the show the quiet-mannered Boston businessman, or the sedate politician (some of them used to come three or four times a week), sauntered their way from the Howard to City Hall via the Bell in Hand pub for a "quickie" while the burlesque devotee of more moderate means quaffed his lager beer at any of the many Scollay Square bars.

Boston's famed Scollay Square is gone and with it the wonderful and wicked Old Howard.

GRAY'S HALL – SOUTHIE'S
LITTLE FANEUIL HALL
(circa 1912)

On November 23, 1880, a group of South Boston residents met to draw up resolutions for a civic organization to be named the City Point Improvement Association. In February, 1893, the name was changed to that of the South Boston's Citizens Association, the first meeting being held in Gray's Hall at the southeast corner of Broadway and I Street. Many improvements stand as monuments to the efforts of the group: the extension of L Street to Boston Proper; the building of South Boston High School and the famous L Street Bathhouse and the majestic Washington Monument atop Dorchester Heights. Evacuation Day observances with Saint Patrick's Day festivities each March 17th are held under auspices of the SBCA. One of its most colorful bunting bedecked observances held in 1912 featured President William Howard Taft as a parade participant and guest of Boston's Mayor, John F. (Honey Fitz) Fitzgerald.

Here, too, shortly after the turn of the century—one flight up, the Imperial moving picture theatre flourished with the introduction of the "flickers." The anguished trials of Pearl White and Elmo Lincoln along with the comic antics of Charlie Chaplin and Fatty Arbuckle brought delight and excitement to Southie. Vaudeville at the "Imp" highlighted Saturday matinee and evening shows. The appreciative audiences asked only that the vaudevillian have a minimum of talent, maximum of nerve and the ability to memorize 15 minutes of monologue and a singing voice loud enough to be heard by passersby on Broadway. Comedian Bennie Drohan, creator of the world famous song "Southie Is My Home Town," first started his professional career at the old Imperial movie palace.

On a Saint Patrick's Day in 1954, State Senator John E. Powers in behalf of the SBCA proclaimed Benjamin Vincent Drohan as "South Boston's Ambassador of Goodwill." Said the senator, "Bennie Dro-

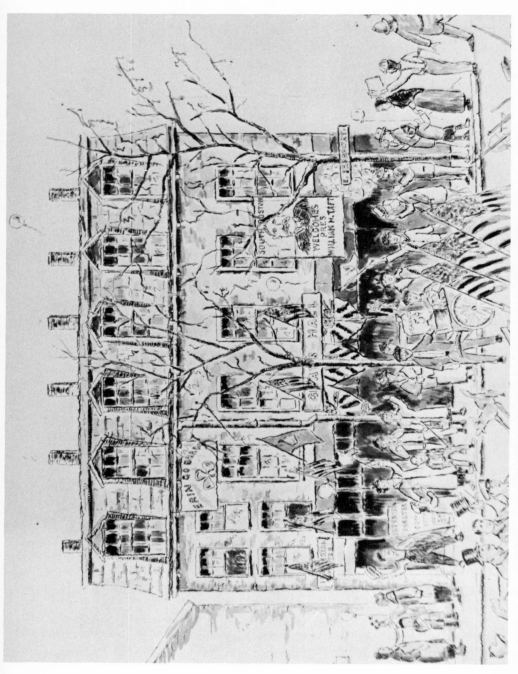

Southie's Little Faneuil Hall — Gray's Hall

han, a native of South Boston, kindly of heart, sympathetic and understanding in misfortune, has distinguished himself in a manner which has earned him the love, respect and esteem of all Southie."

SOUTHIE IS MY HOME TOWN

I had an argument the other day—
With a guy from Oskaloo,
He was braggin' 'bout his old home town;—
Says I to him, "What to do."
I got hot—right under the collar,
To that scholar I did holler.

Chorus (Brightly and Rhythmic)

I was born down on "A" Street, raised up on "B" Street,
"Southie Is My Home Town—"
There's something about it, permit me to shout it,
They're the tops for miles around.
We have doctors and scrappers, preachers and flappers,
Men from the old County Down.—
Say, they'll take you and break you, but they'll never forsake you—
In "Southie My Home Town."*

Southie Is My Home Town — Bennie Drohan

SOUTHIE IS MY HOME TOWN

A century and a quarter ago our national hymn "America" was born. Written by Samuel Francis Smith, a Baptist clergyman, it was first publicly sung in Boston at a Fourth of July celebration in 1831. It was sung that same year by Sunday School children in the Park Street Church across the street from the historic Boston Common.

Oliver Wendell Holmes, a Harvard classmate of Smith, attributes the genius in "America" to its very first word "MY" a personal possessive which instantly strikes a responsive chord in every patriot's heart.

"MY country, 'tis of thee."

"That little pronoun did it all, and will do it forever," said Holmes, brilliant poet and keenist wit of his generation. "That puts 'America' in the hearts of the people, and because of it Sam Smith will live when Longfellow and Whittier and all the rest of us have gone into oblivion."

"Popular music is an index to the life and history of a nation. . . . The manners, customs and current events of every generation have been given expression in popular songs," said Sigmund Spaeth, in his introduction to *A History of Popular Music in America*.

With the start of the Civil War in 1861, came many patriotic songs and hymns and Fort Warren in Boston Harbor was the birthplace of the greatest of them all. The famous Yankee song, "John Brown's Body," was the inspirational song of the 2nd Infantry or Tiger Battalion and first sung while the men were quartered at the fort. Singing seemed to be the best way for the battalion to pass the time away and the singing of the popular songs of the time resulted in a really fine chorus. The favorite hymn "Say Brothers, Will You Meet Us?" sung time and again became the melody chosen by the composers of "John Brown's Body." The music was only slightly changed.

The man who led the raid on Harper's Ferry in 1859 had a Scottish namesake in the Tiger Battalion. He was twitted by his mates that he couldn't be John Brown, for John Brown's body was "a mouldering in the grave." John, himself, helped compose the song that was published in May, 1861. Later, when the famous 14th Regiment left Fort Warren and had departed for Washington, Abraham Lincoln and Julia Ward Howe (wife of the famous Dr. Sam Howe of the Perkins Institute for the Blind in South Boston) visited the camp of the Massachusetts soldiers. The stirring strains so moved the President that he asked Julia Ward Howe to compose a hymn from the tune. "The Battle Hymn of the Republic" was his inspired answer: "Mine eyes have seen the glory of the coming of the Lord."

The North went wild everywhere the magical strains of the song were sung, and the stirring message of the hymn was undoubtedly an inspirational factor in the North's winning the Civil War.

South Boston, heartland of European immigrants, especially of its New England Irish, have for decades given expression to a community pride in one particular song, in which the genius of a native-born Southie songwriter combined the observations of Mr. Holmes, Mrs. Howe and Mr. Spaeth into a simple tune whose jingling verses have intrigued listeners the world over.

"I was born down on A Street. . .Southie is MY home town" they joyously sing at their social or political gatherings all the while the halls resound with melodious conviviality. "Down at the corner of F Street and Third—that's MY home town!" And once again, that personal little pronoun MY puts heart, soul and nostalgic history into a song which captures and solidifies an entire exceptional community.

South Bostonians have sung their old home town songs composed by one of their own, "ever since Hector was a pup." For many years they have urged that their nostalgic tunes composed and harmonized by Southie's lyric songster Bennie Drohan and made famous the world over, be preserved in a home town memorabilia.

Recently, a popular, young Southie accordion musician flew to Ireland to visit relatives he had never seen before. On his arrival, he was entertained in true Irish fashion; then when the high spirits of conviviality called for music, an Irish "cordeen" was pressed upon him and he was urged to favor the audience with a few "Yankee tunes." In fine spirit he broke out with "Southie is my home town." Immediately all his Irish relatives arose from their chairs and stood up! Perplexed, he questioned his Aunt Nora after the completion of his musicale as to why everybody arose when he first began the tune.

"My dear b'y," she answered, "we arlways git oop in repect w'en our Yankee coosins play wan o' their national anthems—why do ye ask lad—aren't we supposed to?"

That little word MY is truly the secret of the nostalgic toe-tripping ditty that tunefully sets each and every individual Southie son or daughter apart—and yet, gathers them all together harmoniously in spirit and song, "Say, they'll take you and break you, but they'll never forsake you, in Southie MY home town."

Admittedly, the song brags. And sometimes the verses are ridiculed by outlanders as being vainglorious and that is understandable. But what does a disservice to the intent of the well-meaning songwriter and joy to millions, deserves better.

Bennie Drohan's career as Southie's Ambassador of Good Will first started its course on ol' Broadway, the town's main stem. For most Southie youngsters at the turn of the century, weekdays were primarily spent in school and at homework. Sunday—church day—saw everything closed up tight. But, Saturdays were paydays for Dad and a dime begged and spent wisely could set up an afternoon of sheer delight. Half the dime went on a bag of "speckles" (over-ripe bananas) from Joe Banana's vegetable stand on Broadway, or for a nickel's worth of stale fudge bought next door at the 5 and 10. The five cents left over was intended for the gala event of the afternoon—the movies! And it was here, on Broadway's three pioneer movie palaces, the Imperial Theatre, the Olympia, and the Congress Hall that young Bennie Drohan first got the musical bug.

The Imperial Theatre, formerly Gray's Hall, at the corner of I Street and Broadway, was owned by Mike Lydon, who hailed from the City Point section of Southie. When the "movie palaces" suddenly gained in popularity, shortly after the turn of the century, South Boston's entertainment entrepreneur, who also ran other theatres and dance halls locally and in Dorchester, combined vaudeville along with the "flickers."

Vaudeville, all during this time, was the popular entertainment vehicle that brought happiness and excitement to Southie. Up until about 1925—the two-and-three-a-day endless stream of flamboyant vaudevillians buncoed their way into entertainment-hungry hearts with merriment, song, laughter and tears. The appreciative audience enjoyed them all. There were singing, dancing and acrobatic routines.

The animal acts that accompanied the vaudeville tours, ranged from the magician's secretly pocketed rabbit to the highly visible dancing elephant, the speaking dog, the educated goose, the trained flea, the boxing kangaroo, and the cornet-tooting musical seal busting up the show with an amazing rendition of "My Country 'tis of Thee."

Then there were the agile acrobatic tricks: bicyclists rode taut wire, buxom tight-rope walkers tripped the light fantastic daintily in mid-air; a six-foot high, accordion-pleated female contortionist tucked her frame away neatly in a two-by-two cask. Musicians shrilled difficult operatic concertos on penny whistles and as a change of finesse, rippled vulgar ditties on the keys of a grand piano. Then, too, there were bald-headed female impersonators, phony bosomed, bewigged and daintily mincing out with falsetto sound—and here again, there were male impersonators, de-bosomed, booming "asleep on the deep" in simulated basso-profundo, to the open-mouthed perplexity and wonderment of Southie's small-fry.

To the average South Boston kid of the golden era, "racism" meant buffoonery, something crudely expressed by actors on the stage and then happily left there. The audience delighted in the antics of the garishly dressed Irish, Jewish, Italian or black-faced comedians—or any other nationality to which an exaggerated brogue or dialectical lingo added to the humor of their monologues or repartee. The corny "give and take"; the pokes, the ribbing—each dig received with high glee and derisive laughter—the sharper the jibe, the bigger the laugh. From this magical cornucopia of ribald corn, small-time vaudeville offered dubious fortune, fickle fame—but most important—uproarious fun.

During the summer lay-off season, the Imperial and the other two Southie theatres, Congress Hall and the Olympia, had no way of keeping the shuttered theatres and their patrons cool outside of the bamboo fans supplied free to "adults only." Small-time Boston vaudevillians and their wives "vacationed" the hot summer away at Carson Beach or at the L Street Bathhouse. Instead of supplying the usual vaudeville acts that required stage lighting, theatre managers kept the theatre darkened and thereby supposedly cooler. The entertainment was supplied by the patrons of the local movies themselves.

Many of Southie's old timers recall with a chuckle that thrill-filled moment when the wildly cheered piano player, always 20 minutes late, finally arrived to plunk her 220 lbs. on the piano stool to open the show at the "Imp." At the first tinkle of the battered old "Baby-grand" a slide flashed on the screen with the request that "Ladies Please Remove Your Hats." After which the lyrics of the latest song hits flashed on the darkened stage where, under the baton of a local songbird, Southie's kids joined in the singing of the era's most popular songs. "I'm Afraid to Go Home in the Dark," was a prime favorite. "Come Josephine In My Flying Machine" was an invitation to the young lady of the lyrics to go "up higher" and "come see the moon on fire." After about fifteen minutes of singing, the exuberant youngsters were calmed down enough for a couple of hours of watching bow-legged "Bronco Billy" clad in colorful wooly chaps, as he and his Annie Oakley-type cowgirl sweetheart popped off charging redskins.

Singing and the joy thereof, was an inexpensive hobby among Southie youngsters whose hard working parents could afford little more or nothing else. For the most part, the songs taught the kids in school were of a patriotic nature and the children needed little prompting to sing them well. The few religious songs and Christmas carols taught were dutifully sung, but it was the lively popular songs of the day that the kids enjoyed singing and storing away in their minds for years to come. The boy and girl who had a "voice" or who could play a piano to liven up a Southie party, or who were blessed with talent and strong wind to blow a harmony on a harmonica at a "doorstep tunefest" never lacked friends or invitations to the local socials. Quite often, it was a congeniality of Irish wit and song that started a successful career on its way, not necessarily that of a professional entertainer, but in political life. Many a young "pol" started his way up the ladder by singing off the back of a beer wagon while waiting his turn to address a street corner political rally.

Bennie Drohan was that sort of a happy-go-lucky Southie lad. His rollicking way with a tune and his Irish wit was a pleasure to hear and behold. Even as a schoolboy he had learned by carefully observing local talent the artful knack of sparkling one's own personality. He loved Southie, sang joyously for it and about it, and as he became more proficient in his talent, made friends and admirers prodigiously.

Boston slowly began replacing the old type movie palaces from the very beginning of the jazzy 20's and when finally Southie's new Broadway Theatre opened its doors with a higher grade of entertainment, young Drohan was on hand to spark the cast of vaudeville stars. It was a happy day for the young entertainer and his beloved bride whom he had met for the first time at the "Broadway" when they teamed up to produce their own show later known as Marty Dupree's Follies. The talented and attractive young couple had a beautiful "hand in hand marriage." Both loved the "show biz" and the work they had set themselves out to do. Bennie was creative—but it was Marty who was the mainstay. She adored her "B. V. D." and boosted the baggy-pants comedian and his knack with music to the very stars and it was early in their married life when Bennie's rollicking immortal song was first introduced to a wildly delighted and receptive Southie audience. And it all couldn't have come at a better time!

Southie's nostalgic tune hit the entertainment field when big band music was at its height and radio proved a bonanza for fresh song hits and a sounding board for local and untried comedians. Southie flappers and their cake-eater beaus danced to the Charleston at open-air block dances every Wednesday night in various sections of the hometown. And everywhere and always Bennie and his "Southie" sparked every dance, every good and happy time.

It was also the time of "The Great Depression," along with its ignominious running mate "Prohibition." But Southie took the lack of jobs and beer in its usual cheery manner and made the most of hard times. After all, bologna at depression prices at two pounds for a quarter made up a couple of "dozen poverty sandwiches" and the remaining seventy-five cents left out of the buck, bought a can of hop-flavored malt, a yeast cake and five pounds of sugar. The resulting concoction—five gallons of homebrew (properly aged for a period of a week), the sandwiches and a huge pot of South Boston baked beans were all the ingredients necessary to properly celebrate a happy Paddy's Day evening.

"To hell with poverty" was toasted, an accordion was summoned, the fourteen ounce empty jam glasses were colored with the white foam of Mulcahey's golden nectar and the party roared out with "Southie Is My Home Town!"

The neighbors hearing the sound of "Southie" knew there was a good time in the making and came "troopin" in with their "party donations" and then for sure the rafters rang with song and the floorboards creaked under dancing feet.

BENJAMIN V. DROHAN AND
MARGARET E. DROHAN

...REQUIESCAT...

Benjamin V. Drohan, 77, composer of the well-known South Boston tune—*Southie Is My Home Town*—died April 24, 1972 in a Boston Hospital after a long illness. Born and raised in South Boston, Bennie Drohan spent his life in show business, beginning with local minstrel shows and moving into vaudeville and musical comedy. On October 28, the same year, his beloved wife also died in a Boston Hospital after a prolonged illness. Bennie Drohan performed for several decades with his wife, Margaret McCarthy Drohan, whose stage name was Marty Dupree. The couple starred in vaudeville shows on the Loews and Keith circuit and headed a tabloid show that featured two dozen performers. During World War II Bennie and Marty danced, performed and sang *Southie* for the USO in the front lines of battle. They performed for servicemen in Belgium during the Battle of the Bulge and in England during the Blitz. In Korea, the couple gladdened the hearts of homesick GI's with *Southie*. Bennie was a frequent singer and performer at political rallies for James Michael Curley, late mayor of Boston and governor of Massachusetts. In his later years he was an assistant public relations director at Rockingham Park in New Hampshire, where he arranged and performed in several charity shows. He was a constant member of the L Street Brownies. A requiem Mass was sung April and October in St. Gregory's Church, Dorchester. Burial was in St. Mary's Cemetery, Dorchester, Mass.

Pastoral South Boston — "Precious Memorabilia"

PASTORAL SOUTH BOSTON

(circa 1820)

Beautiful indeed was the South Boston peninsula of the early settlers' days with its green rolling hills, meadows and orchards. The thirty-six lush acres lying between Dorchester, Third, Old Harbor and G Streets belonged to Oliver Wiswell. Dorchester Heights (the Twin Hills) overlooking Dorchester Bay were owned by Messrs. Wiswell and Bird. Thomas Bird, beginning in 1677, had over a period of years accumulated some thirty acres bounded by the Old Road (Emerson Street) on the North and Old Harbor on the South, running from G to I Streets. The road to Fort Independence (then Castle William, which was built in 1633) took the line of the present Dorchester Street to Emerson, then passed into East Fourth Street to City Point.

In 1805, the Dorchester and Milton Turnpike (now Dorchester Avenue) was built by a private corporation, and extended along the marsh from the Boston South Bridge to Lower Mills. There was a tollhouse and gate at the bridge, and also on what is now Preble Street at Andrew Square in the Washington Village section, "where tolls, established by law, were collected for all carts, wagons and individuals who used the Turnpike." Both avenues of approach improved the flow of commerce into the peninsula.

Many wealthy and prominent Boston Brahmin built beautiful estates with magnificent gardens and orchards on what is now Broadway and, in the course of events, they developed business enterprises on the peninsula, particularly in the section of the waterfront facing the parent city.

In the early history of South Boston, settlers were obliged to attend church services in neighboring Dorchester, as there were not enough residents to support a minister. When South Boston became annexed to Boston, Mr. John Hawes, a public-spirited citizen, appropriated land in 1807 on which the first house for public worship was erected. In 1810, Hawes joined with neighbors in erecting a church building, and the Rev. Thomas Pierce, a clergyman of the Methodist denomination was employed as minister. Originally the Hawes Place Church until 1892, it was later occupied as an art school.

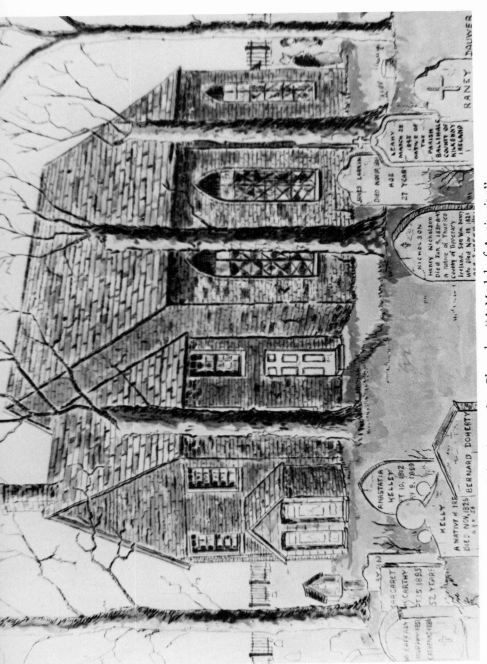

Saint Augustine Chapel — "A Model of Antiquity"

SAINT AUGUSTINE CHAPEL

"A Model of Antiquity"

Bishop John Cheverus purchased in 1818 the land off Dorchester Street that now constitutes Saint Augustine Cemetery. Immediately after its purchase, a small building, later used as a chapel, was erected and within this structure the remains of the Rev. Francis Matigon, for twenty-six years Pastor of the Church of the Holy Cross in Boston, a French exile, and many of the earliest of Boston's Irish Catholics were interred. The names and dates on the ancient tombstones remind visitors, especially those of Irish descent, of the link between the historic chapel and the history of the early-day Irish in Boston.

In 1833, the chapel became too small to accommodate the growing numbers of worshippers and a new building in South Boston had to be erected. In 1845, a new church dedicated to SS Peter and Paul replaced the old Saint Augustine Chapel, supplemented a few years later by the Gate of Heaven Church in 1863. In 1868, through the spiritual guidance of the Rev. Denis O'Callaghan, the chapel was re-opened and in the small quarters the parishioners gathered, and it was here that plans were made for a new church. In September of 1870, the cornerstone of the present Saint Augustine Church was laid, with the first Mass said in the basement in July, 1871, and on August 30, 1874, the dedication rites were performed by Archbishop Williams.

In preparation for the Boston bicentennial celebration, The Committee for the Restoration of Saint Augustine Cemetery in 1975 conducted a major fund-raising drive for the extensive structural repair work necessary in the historic chapel, and for the beautification of the Cemetery Yard. A model of antiquity, the chapel and cemetery was registered as a national historic landmark with a plaque to that effect.

Perkins School For the Blind

MINE EYES HAVE SEEN THE GLORY

(circa 1890)

(They First Saw The Light In South Boston)
Perkins School for the Blind
H Street and Broadway, South Boston

As early as the turn of the nineteenth century, Southie's excellent recreational facilities and wide beaches began to attract Boston's carriage trade as a summer resort area. Only a short half hour travel by horse-drawn vehicles from Beacon Hill brought the heat-relief-seeking Brahmin to the fashionable Mount Washington Hotel at Broadway and H Street, on top of the Twin Hill. Erected in 1834, the rambling six-storied brick structure sheltered the proper Bostonians during their summer sojourns. Before its demolition previous to the First World War, the building was occupied by the world famous Perkins School for the Blind (1839-1912) for a span of seventy-three years.

Among the Perkins School's most illustrious pupils "that first saw the light in South Boston" were the world famous Laura Bridgman, Helen Keller and Anne Sullivan. Directors Samuel Gridley Howe and Michael Anagnos were major factors in the success of these remarkable blind women. While Dr. Howe was director of the school, his wife, Julia Ward Howe, at the request of President Abraham Lincoln, wrote the words of the inspired song "The Battle Hymn of the Republic."

Although the Perkins School moved to Watertown in 1912, the workshop where the community's blind men and women could develop specific skills remained at the rambling corner house on top of G Street, directly opposite the South Boston High School, until 1952.

"They first saw the light in South Boston."

First South Boston Bridge — "Bridge of Sighs"

BRIDGE OF SIGHS

(circa 1810)

First South Boston Bridge

"Ship-to-shore" marketing on the South Boston Bridge (now the Dover Street Bridge) is shown during the height of its popularity.

When Southie (Mattapanock in Indian) was annexed to Boston, its native Yankees, shortly followed by Erin's sons and daughters, began streaming over the newly-built connecting bridge. In 1803, the peninsula was bought from its early settlers as a real estate speculation. The result of this manipulation and the arrival of the Irish prompted the town fathers of Boston, in 1804, to receive "Southie" into the township.

The wooden pile bridge from its very beginning became the Boston Beaus' favorite promenade. Sketches, drawn by various artists of the time, depict parading femininity arm in arm with their blue-blooded dandies pictured within a panorama of Boston Towne against a colorful array of roofs, steeples and ships' rigging. The bridge and its approaches were used extensively by pedestrians, and beginning early evenings, without the disturbances of mounted riders or wagons, it became a rendezvous for sweethearts and was romantically referred to as "The Bridge of Sighs."

Romance and commerce flourished in a sprightly fashion because of improved methods of access to the little peninsula. The main pathway from Dorchester to the Point (now Emerson to E. Fourth Street, which had originally been trodden down hard by cattle going daily to and from pasture, became in time a public street path. But it was the hangman's noose on days of public executions that brought thousands of morbid gapers from Boston over bridge and pike to swell the toll-keepers' coffers. Beginning in 1812, public executions took place in South Boston.

Monday Morning Snowman — Rear of 134 M Street, South Boston

MONDAY MORNING SNOWMAN

(circa 1916)

Sketched from "out my window," rear of 134 M Street
in South Boston. Backyard tenement scene recalls
many childhood memories.

It was just after the War of 1812 when South Boston began taking the first steps toward high density population with the introduction of row houses, whole streets of houses of identical design, no space between them and just a patch of land in the rear. The "yard" served as an area for the covered shed containing the tenants' ash and swill barrels. A large pole jutting upwards from the rear of the yard, with attached pulley-lines for "hanging of the wash," served as many as six housewives.

The tenement, or the so-called three-decker, got its name from the three verandas which first appeared in the front of the better type house and which later were moved to the back. They provided a middle area between the poor and the middle-class with their many-roomed single family dwellings. The construction of the tenements was facilitated by the development of balloon-framing which followed the mass production of cheaper nails in 1817. As a result, South Boston was able to grow with unbelievable speed.

It was also the time (1912) when the average wage-earner was getting about $500 a year. That was the average, not the minimum. The tenements were then rented on the basis of week to week or month to month, the rent being invariably required in advance. A week's pay was paid for a month's rent. Rents of the time averaged two dollars a week for the poorer type tenement, (lamp light and toilet in the cellar) to $15 a month for five rooms, kitchen-stove heated, inside toilet and gas piped in for lighting, which deluxe South Boston realtors, Spinny and Kelly, classified as "all improvements."

"Last Stop - City Point" — City Point - Bay View Trolley

LAST STOP – CITY POINT

(circa 1912)

City Point – Head House – Castle Island – Pleasure Bay

The strong ties between South Boston and the North End became aligned when Boston's population growth soared during the Civil War. Boston's war industry drew upon the North End's Irish and Italians to lay the tracks for the "hoss cars," dig sewer trenches for the foundry and hasten the sorely needed row tenements.

When Southie progressed to the electric car lines, the old "Bay-View" traversed Eighth Street alongside Dorchester Bay, up K Street and then along Sixth Street to City Point. The last of the open-air trolleys had a top speed of six miles an hour. A five-cent fare brought as many as 70,000 Bostonians of a golden summer day to flock the three-mile ocean resort area of the peninsula. The beaches at the famous old Head House and Castle Island (Pleasure Bay) offered local salt-water enthusiasts and its daily thousands of summer visitors (doughnut democrats) a resort area where every sort of aquatic sport or outdoor conviviality was made available. Loaded down with bags of doughnuts, sandwiches and sundry articles of beach paraphernalia, they scattered round and about to the many attractions of their choice. For fifty cents spent at the Peninsula Hotel veranda bar Uncle Mike could achieve a "Sunday glow" (three 16 oz. lager beers and a double hooker) that lasted well up to closing time.

The Walt Disney architectural embellishment of the Head House was suggested by a structure erected by the German government at the World Fair in 1893. At the turn of the century, South Boston had a large German-American citizenry. Summer Sunday afternoons and evenings on the large restaurant balcony, a fine German band would serenade Boston's music lovers and "lovers."

The beloved structure was named "Head House" because it was at the "head" of Boston's peninsula, jutting out "ahead" into Boston Harbor. On December 5, 1942, flames of undetermined origin destroyed the famous structure and the blaze quickly spread to the pier that juts out into the Harbor.

Kelly's Landing — "Sailing Chicks"

KELLY'S LANDING

(circa 1911)

"Sailing Chicks"

The several yacht clubs: Columbia, Boston, South Boston, Puritan Yacht Club and the Mosquito (the latter demolished), perched alike to mother hens at water's edge, have for the past one hundred years sent out thousands of sailing chicks to skim the waters of scenic Dorchester Bay. Promenaders, from early morn to late evenings stroll Day Boulevard (named after Judge Day, Louise Day Hicks' illustrious father) all eager for a snack of Kelly's reknown fried clams prepared at the restaurant adjacent to the Public Boat Landing, ready to leave the landing for a delightful harbor view cruise. Marine Park and City Point at the tip of the South Boston peninsula was the summer resort area of thousands of Boston's "doughnut democrats." The fishing from off the pier stretching out into Boston Harbor from Castle Island is both enjoyable and rewarding.

In 1874, at the earnest solicitation of several influential members of the then newly established Boston Yacht Club, the firm of George Lawley & Son Corporation were induced to bring their boat-building facilities to City Point. George Lawley, an English ship-builder and his son established their shop on the property of the Boston Yacht Club on Sixth Street, near the foot of P Street. A few years later, the Lawley Yards were moved to the north and harbor side of South Boston.

The shipyard of George Lawley had a national reputation. The Messrs Lawley constructed the racing yachts for Thomas W. Lawson, world famous maritime sportsman.

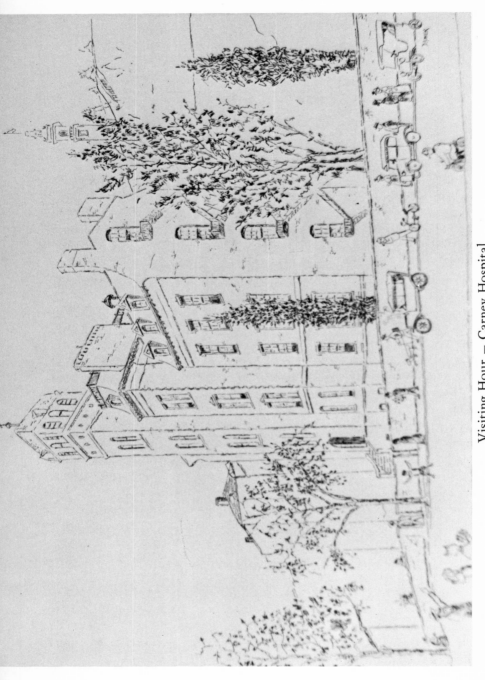

Visiting Hour – Carney Hospital

VISITING HOUR

Carney Hospital, Dorchester Heights

(circa 1918)

In 1863, Andrew Carney a well-to-do Catholic philanthropist purchased the land atop Dorchester Heights where the hospital stood. It was placed under the charge of the Sisters of Charity. The gift of property was made to Sister Ann Alexis, superior of the orphan asylum on Camden Street in Boston. The building, known as the Howe Mansion, outgrew its space and in 1865 plans were drawn for the brick building at a cost of about $100,000. Mr. Carney contributed $75,000.

The beloved Carney abdicated its high-perched throne of mercy on Old Harbor Street in 1945 when, under the inspired help of Southie's Prince of the Church, Cardinal Cushing, a rebuilt edifice now serves the hospital's former patients with ultra-modern accommodations in the neighboring suburb of Dorchester.

Before the days of "the Great Depression," the doors of the accident ward were open all hours of the day to the distressed Southie parents with bruised, cut, or ailing kids requiring emergency treatment. Tens of thousands of South Boston's folks found aid and kindness at the hands of the Carney's good doctors, nurses and nuns.

Sister Gabriel, one recalls, presided over the "Outpatient Clinic" with the combined tyranny of a despotic martinet and the sublime charity of the Blessed Mother. Most endearing of all, perhaps, was the characteristic method the old Southie nun used in her urgency to assist the ailing. "Come-come dearie!" stirred doctor and nurse to a renewed and continuing degree of efficiency. All of which finally earned the little saint her reward in heaven.

The charitable spirit of the wee nun lingers on in the inspired efforts of the good sisters of Marion Manor that continue to care for the aged and the infirm in a revised section of the old Carney. The blended aroma of ether and iodine, seemingly as of today, still lingers around the emergency entrance on National Street.

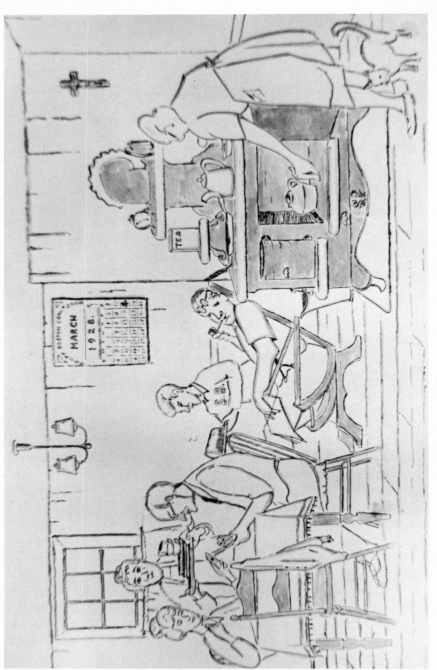

Saturday Night Supper – South Boston

SATURDAY NIGHT SUPPER

(circa 1928)

Beans, beans, the musical fruit
The more you eat—the more you toot!

"Why do we still bake Boston Beans as Hester Friend did in 1649? It is simply because Hester Friend had the secret of real Boston Beans over 325 years ago. Who are we to change it? So we don't." Boston's famous bean recipe goes back to the town's early rootings. This is the claim made by New England's "Friends," the commercial baker of their reknown and succulent product.

Made world famous by Boston's elite and humble alike and justly commemorated in every worthwhile cookbook all over the globe, it is, however, in Boston's suburban South Boston that the earthy, robust baked beans, skillfully blended with mustard, onions and molasses, and then garnished with "a little bit o' love" achieved their succulent peak of perfection through years of mother-to-daughter know-how.

Beantown's Mayor, Kevin White, was the recipient of a card from a Virginia housewife requesting information regarding Boston Beans and the baking method. The mayor, knowing the complexities involved in properly concocting the one and only Boston variety, wisely parried the Virginia bride's request, giving it to a local news page devoted to printing cooking recipes. A Southie great grandmother provided the outlander with the recipe that had banqueted her family for four generations.

When Southie was annexed to Boston in 1804, thousands of Beantown's Yankees began streaming over the then newly-built connecting "Bridge of Sighs," bringing their bean crocks along with them. And, shortly thereafter, when the failure of the potato crop brought the Irish immigrants knocking for admittance at Southie's back door, it was the welcoming aroma of the beanpot that beckoned them in. Where Ireland's spuds had failed—South Boston's beans succeeded.

Southie's housewives sent their pots down to the local corner bakery where, for a nickle—in the good ol' days—, the beans would be baked. The task of delivery was delegated to the school kids, boys and girls alike. Arms filled with schoolbooks and beanpots, they hastened to the nearest bakeshop every Friday morning to unload themselves of their prospective "Saturday night supper." Later, when the pots were gathered up, the exuberant youngsters, in anticipation of a pre-supper bean sandwich on crusty homemade bread, happily joined in song extolling the digestible merits of their cargo—

"Beans, beans, the musical fruit
The more you eat—the more you toot!

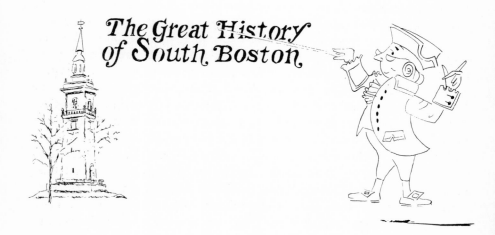

The Great History of South Boston

THE ORIGINAL SOUTH BOSTON
SAVINGS BANK BUILDING
(circa 1863)

"Gentlemen, our community has come of age"

With these words of inspiration a group of South Boston residents moved a need into a reality and, on September 1, 1863, the doors of the South Boston Savings availed the community the means of employing their money to advantage. As the community grew, with its businesses and homes, the bank became a vital, living part of the area providing financial advice and leadership. Through six depressions the South Boston Savings Bank assisted homeowners and businessmen alike to maintain their homes and livelihoods and earn the respect and title of "good neighbor." The bank now occupies the bright modern building at West Broadway near Dorchester Street.

For well over one century, the civic-minded institution has to an extraordinary extent given of its time and resources to promote and memorialize the historical events that have perpetuated South Boston's history. This effort has focused largely on the Bicentennial period, 1776-1976. The bank's dedicated efforts were rewarded when Mr. Alfred W. Archibald, President of the institution, was notified that the bank had been named recipient of the George Washington Honor Medal Award by the Freedoms Foundation at Valley Forge, Pennsylvania for 1971, advertising *The Great History of South Boston Series.* The illustrated series comprised eight historical events relative to South Boston, bicentennial 1776, and were all published in Boston and South Boston's principal newspapers:

1. South Boston Savings Bank
   "An historical monument to security!"
2. "L Street" — Its Bathhouse and Its Brownies!!
3. History marches by on the streets of South Boston!
   Evacuation Day Parade
4. Knox: a rough trip to South Boston!
   Henry Knox, Patriot

The Original South Boston Savings Bank

5. Security: Circa 1634
   Castle Island
6. What's Dorchester Heights doing in South Boston?
   Dorchester Heights
7. South Boston's wooden ships and iron men
   The Northern Light
8. They first saw the light in South Boston
   Perkins School For the Blind — 1880

"An outstanding accomplishment in helping to achieve a better understanding of Americans and America."

The South Boston Branch Library, established in 1872, remained in its location in the old bank building at W. Broadway and E Street for 86 years. Of the original book collection of 4,360 volumes, 1470 had been donated by the Mattapan Literary Association, a group of young Southies established in 1848 "for the mutual improvement of its members in literary accomplishments." On October 31, 1957 the library moved to its permanent building on the site of the old Lincoln School at East Broadway.

The illustrious South Boston School of Art was maintained in the upper hall of the bank building. In 1870, the school was moved to Hawes Place Church at the corner of Emerson and K Streets.

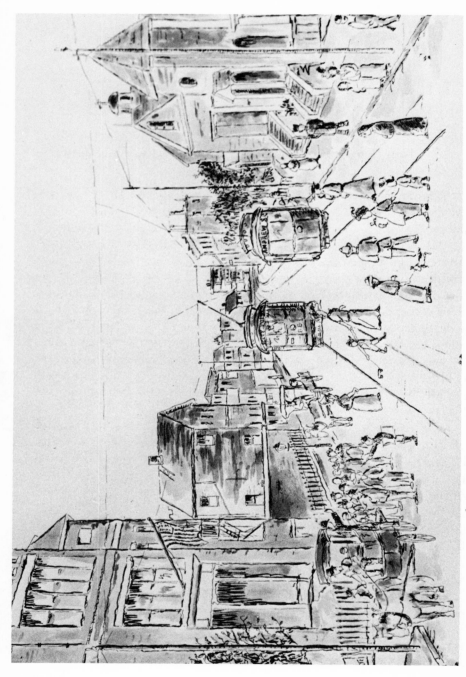

Andrew Square – Washington Village – John W. McCormack

I REMEMBER WHEN I WAS THIRTEEN
John W. McCormack

Andrew Square, Washington Village, South Boston.
(circa 1912)

"I remember when I was thirteen. I was interested in politics even then. I loved to attend street corner rallies and listen to the politicians.

"My brother and I had a newspaper route on Vinton Street near Andrew Square in South Boston. We worked hard to help our dear wonderful mother put food on the table"—to quote Speaker John W. McCormack on a Saint Patrick's Day TV program in Boston. "When I went into politics, my customers remembered me." He was elected a delegate to the Massachusetts Constitutional Convention in 1917. When his father, a bricklayer, died, he became the man of the house. "I had to quit school, I was never able to attend high school or college.

"Mr. Way, my employer, encouraged me to read law, and he made his law books available to me."

McCormack passed the Massachusetts Bar examination at the age of 21. When World War I broke out, he enlisted in the army. Later he served in the Massachusetts House of Representatives from 1920 to 1922 and in the State Senate for three years. In 1928, the voters of the 12th Congressional District sent him to Congress. He remained until his retirement in 1970.

"Yes, Cardinal Cushing and I were good friends. He enjoyed politics and was a good listener. Years ago, I told his Eminence that had he chosen politics in his youth, he would have easily been sitting where I am today."

Strangely enough, both the Speaker and the Cardinal resembled each other to a remarkable extent. Not only in appearance—but in a highly moral and religious degree. Both took an understandable pride in their Irish Catholic heritage and in the South Boston community they were born and raised in.

In Washington, the Capital of the United States, they called him the "Archbishop" behind his back, and he resented it. Despite his close association with Southern Democrats, McCormack was a strong civil rights advocate. He was cordial towards the Jewish community, and his first appointment to the Naval Academy was a Jewish youth.

"Next to God and Mrs. McCormack," said the Speaker of the House of Representatives, "I love most the House of Representatives."

For John W. McCormack of South Boston it was the day of last hurrahs. After being showered with compliments for more than two hours, the aging statesman finally ended a lengthy career in Congress (forty-two years) and his nine years as its Speaker.

He received a standing ovation from the members present, then walked slowly to the platform, smiled, and gavelled the house to silence one last time. It was Majority Leader Carl Albert (D-Okla.), who had labored in McCormack's shadow and then replaced him as Speaker of the House of Representatives, who gave the retiring Congressman a most special place in history.

"McCormack," Albert said, "represented the rise of the Irish to political power only two generations after they arrived in the United States. Isolated physically and intellectually for more than a half of a century, they had been roused from their lethargy by men like McCormack."

The day in 1962 when McCormack took the gavel in the U. S. House of Representatives was the fulfillment of a lifetime of labor and dreams. An Irish striver, who had supported his fatherless family and raised himself from the meanest poverty of South Boston, he was the first Roman Catholic ever elected Speaker. He had worked and waited with loyalty and patience under the patronage and shadow of Sam Rayburn for more than three decades. Finally, he achieved the rostrum once held by Clay and Cannon, Clark and Longworth.

The plaque beneath the portrait of McCormack in the main lobby of the building which dominates Post Office Square in Boston official-ly proclaims the structure to be the John W. McCormack Post Office and Courthouse.

"I want to thank my colleagues in the Congress for the act naming this building in honor of me," McCormack said, "I have a little personal feeling. I'm glad they did it while I'm alive."

McCormack said such an occasion could only happen in one place. "I certainly never thought of such a thing when I was a kid in Andrew Square and roaming around South Boston," he said, "it is only in America that this could happen."

McCormack added, "we should welcome the time of challenge we live in, and that the United States will emerge from it with renewed strength.

"I have every confidence in that," he said, "the spirit of America is just as strong today as it ever has been in the past. . . .We should separate these kind of people, those who do good things, from the two or three percent of people who do bad things. . .I'm never going to cease my activity in public affairs."

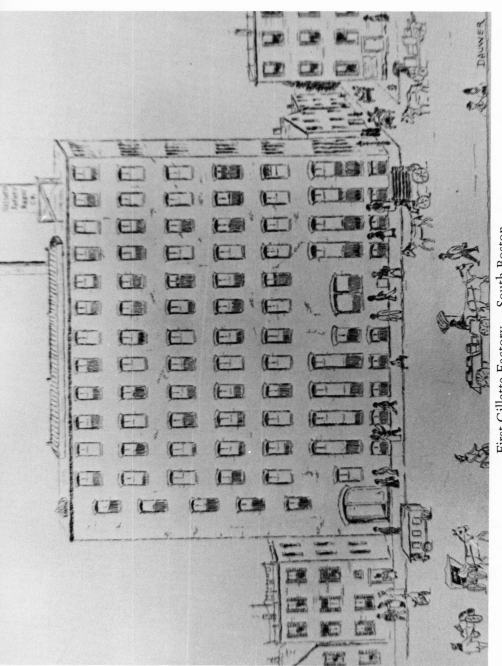

First Gillette Factory — South Boston

FIRST GILLETTE FACTORY

(South Boston - circa 1905)

From Beard to Beardless—An Horatio Alger True Life Story

Changing the face of mankind in the space of a few years is a pretty broad claim to make. It is a fact, however, that from the dawn of civilization no radical advances had been made in the method of removing the hirsute growth from the face of man until the inventive genius of King C. Gillette gave to the world a safety razor that made shaving easy, comfortable, safe, inexpensive and popular.

"The day of its inception I went to Wilkinson's, a hardware store on Washington Street, Boston, and purchased pieces of brass, some steel ribbon used for clock springs, a small hand vise, some files and with these materials made the first razor. . . .

"So it went for nearly six years, during which I was experimenting with blades. . .I tried every cutler and machine shop in Boston and some in New York and Newark in an effort to find someone who knew something about hardening and tempering steel so it would keep its flatness and not be warped by strains.

"If I had been technically trained, I would have quit or probably would never have begun. I was a dreamer who believed in the 'gold at the foot of the rainbow' promise and continued in the path where wise ones feared to tread." And that is the reason why there is a Gillette razor today.

In 1901, Mr. Gillette persuaded some friends to raise the sum of $5,000 to form a company and start manufacturing. In the year 1903, a total of 51 razors and 14 dozen blades were sold for the whole year. The rest is history—men everywhere welcomed the new freedom from whisker bondage and sales leaped ahead year by year. Since the company was formed in South Boston, the Gillette Company has produced well over one-half billion razors and over 115 billion blades in its plants throughout the world.

During 1973, the Gillette Company announced it had signed commitments for 246,000 square footage in the Prudential Center, making possible accommodations for the creation of 500 new jobs in the Boston area.   It tied in with Gillette's plans to expand its world headquarters in Boston's Prudential Center, moving several headquarters and administrative functions from Chicago to Boston.

The company's products and services are sold in more than 170 countries and territories.   It has manufacturing facilities in sixteen countries and sales subsidiaries in nineteen other countries.   The company employs about 27,700 persons worldwide.

BLINSTRUB'S

(circa 1965)

Eat, drink, and be merry, and God bless you all!

Each Thanksgiving Day at Stanley Blinstrub's Village Cafe on South Boston's Broadway, saw Cardinal Cushing host a "November cook-in" for Boston's overlooked senior citizens. "Eat, drink and be merry, and God bless you all!" To prove the analogy, he danced an Irish jig, hand-swinging two delighted older ladies, while an accompanying priest at the piano played Bennie Drohan's endearing tune, "Southie Is My Home Town."

To an old Southie lass at the party, who had just passed her 100th birthday, he kidded: "If I die and get to heaven and you're not there I'll know you're still alive!"

Bennie Drohan, Southie's beloved comedian and songwriter, often performed at Blinstrub's for the various community fund-raising drives. No local talent had to ask Drohan twice for his assistance in freely offering his precious gag material and verses as two other favorite sons of Boston can attest. Jimmy Joyce, often a featured star at Blinstrub's, later became the "Jolly Jester," and, with Frank Fontaine, who starred in Jackie Gleason's TV show, obtained their earliest material from the dusty files and trunks in Bennie's attic.

No, Blinstrub's was no ordinary fun-of-the-mill night club. For to its stage, thousands of Boston's theater-goers had come to delight in Connie Francis at her peak, and time again the lines were stretched to E Street on Broadway when Jimmy Durante, Patti Page and Al Martino drew more than the "main room," a conglomeration of tables and chairs seating near 2,000, could handle. Blinstrub's nostalgic pages bulged with a hundred stage names even into the margins. Sammy Davis, Wayne Newton and Arthur Godfrey's protege Julius LaRosa had used its stage as a springboard to countrywide recognition.

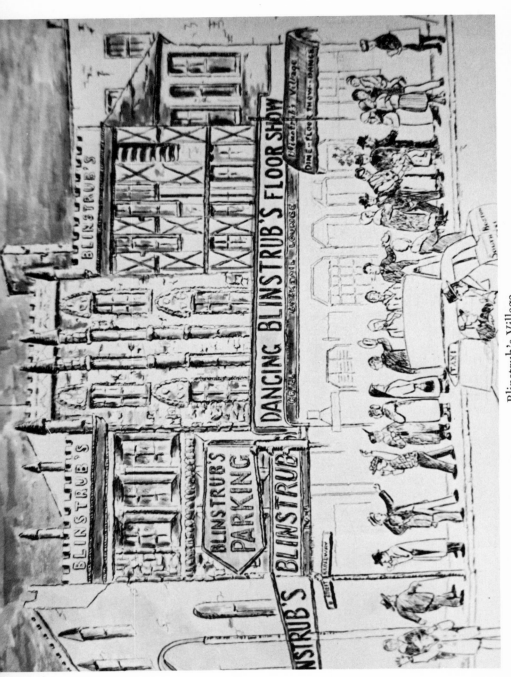

Blinstrub's Village

Long famous as one of America's largest and most popular night clubs, Blinstrub's was destroyed by fire February 7, 1968. While the gaudy painted exterior was presumedly that of a "Belgian Castle," the interior in sharp contrast was handsomely furnished. The structure was a total loss. An era of nostalgic entertainment was ended.

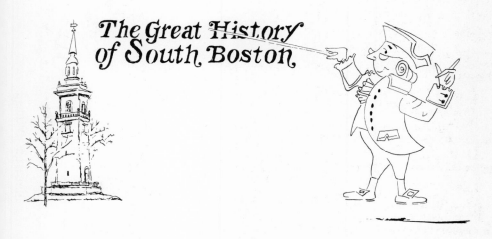

The Great History of South Boston

Sports — A Symbolic Part of the History of South Boston

SPORTS—A SYMBOLIC PART OF THE HISTORY OF SOUTH BOSTON

John Bull narrates that England's military struggles were not won on the battlefields but on the playing fields of Eton. His boast being substantiated by an impressive list of historical victories. There, on Britain's Thames, the English cadet strengthened brawn and stamina in highly competitive sports along with other countrymen in developing the essential physical and mental characteristics necessary to subdue the enemy in battle, and thereby put themselves in a position to impose and collect taxes.

That these highly regarded qualities were not given an opportunity to be displayed by Lord Howe, a former wearer of the Eton jacket, on a certain blustery month of March in 1776, on Dorchester Heights in South Boston, does not in the least detract from the wisdom of his departure by ship from Boston Harbor.

The Continental soldier looking down from on top of the fortified hillock at the departing vessels could little foresee, or dream, that within a few decades, the shore area of Dorchester Bay in Boston Harbor could become a proving ground more famous than the playing areas of Eton, or that the slopes of the hill where their beasts of burden now grazed would become a teeming area catering to the physical, moral and recreational needs of future American patriots and athletes.

"A great deal of talent is lost in the world for want of a little courage," said a Prince of the Church born in the shadow of Dorchester Heights and himself a lover of games, sports and people. . . . Everyday sends to their graves obscure men whose timidity prevented from making a first effort; who, if they could have been induced to begin, would in all probability have gone great lengths in the career of fame. The fact is that to do anything in the world worth doing we must not stand back shivering and thinking of the cold and danger but jump in and scramble through as well as we can."

And who could brag courage any better than the little South Boston lad sans protective football gear playing on a gravel-strewn vacant lot finding a pigskin oval jammed hard into his belly, looks up into eleven scowling young faces and hears the terrifying sound of twenty-two lumbering boots beating down hard in his direction. And when dragged out from under the pile-up, shouts with joy when he sees the football placed behind two empty tomato cans seeing service as goal posts.

Courageous efforts of this sort became part of a boy's character. Indecision, one finds, never placed life's football behind two rewarding tomato cans.

However, let's get back to sports. No sooner had Lord Howe's ocean convoy disappeared from behind Castle Island in Boston Harbor when the little peninsula resumed its job of being Dame Boston's playground. South Boston's many hills and fresh water ponds had even before the Revolutionary War provided Bostonians and its few native "Southies" with perfect arenas for sports, whether of the summer or winter variety, while Dorchester Bay attracted the salt-water enthusiast. Even public hangings for the entertainment of thousands of Boston's spectators were commonplace if that could be misconstrued as being of a recreational value. And besides, the hills were ideal for rolling down barrels of beer to be enjoyed during or after public executions or, again, for picnic hijinks.

Seemingly, of all the four seasons, it was during the bitter cold New England winters that the early-day Bostonians relished games and sports the most. The old pond at the corner of Fourth and G Streets, in the crisp air of winter rung out oftentimes with the merry laughter of "lovey-dovey" skaters, and those at K and Fifth, K and Third, and D and Seventh Streets resounded with the shouts of boys and girls as their hockey sticks once more had the freedom of these arenas to enjoy the best of winter sports.

During these wintry seasons, swiftly gliding iceboats scooted the glary expanse of Dorchester Bay, impelled by wind and freighted with Boston's sportsmen and their dates bent upon having the rarest of sport. Horse races upon the ice furnished prime amusement, and pleasure driving could be a dangerous sport upon the frozen bay. The winter of 1872 witnessed an accident in which a pair of valuable horses were drowned; the owner narrowly escaping a watery grave.

A much safer spit of land for the horse-drawn ice buggies and skaters was found at Boston Neck, a swampy stretch that froze over solid to a mere depth of only two or three feet. Boston Neck, or Roxbury Neck, was the rib of land which connected the parent city with South Boston. Later the trotting races on the snow were transferred to the Mile Ground, Brighton Avenue (now Commonwealth Avenue) between the State Armory and Allston. The charioteers then frequently resorted to the Cattle Fair Hotel where chills were driven off with hot toddies and "Tom and Jerries." The last stronghold of this great winter sport was Beacon Street from St. Mary's to the foot of the rise at Coolidge Corner.

Boston's early-day artists gave ample witness by depicting the various winter sports within a Boston Common background. On a snow-sparkling late afternoon, when school let out, Boston's famous cow pasture became the winter wonderland for young and old alike. The middle-aged and the beginner skated the historic Frog Pond "a la arabesque" or several joined together to "snaketail" off the last in line. The more agile teen-age sportsmen coasted the long Common slopes. The "Long Coast" from the corner of Park and Beacon Street to the West Street entrance and along the Tremont Street Mall was the favorite course, though the Beacon Street Mall, the path from Joy Street, and the hill still dedicated to coasting were also used.

On the Common, particularly on Flagstaff Hill, the doublerunner, or double-ripper came into high popularity by the more spunky of the sledding enthusiasts. Sleds of this type were colorful and often of elaborate make. In the *Boston Globe* for January 27, 1875, the first appearance of the "Highlander" on the Common was described: "It was a long double-runner of the usual pattern, painted red, with a head-light like a juvenile locomotive, and a steering apparatus on the tiller principle. It was cushioned quite elegantly, and has side rests for the feet of the coasters, of whom it will accommodate eight or ten. A large white streamer ornaments the prow, and there are brass trimmings and handles along the sides." The *Boston Herald* of the same day places the cost of the doublerunner at two hundred and fifty dollars. The same item today, provided one could be constructed, would undoubtedly be ten times that of a hundred years ago.

Lads from the North End and South Boston, not to be outdone, constructed their own home-made doublerunners. The "Saint Patrick" made its appearance shortly after that of the Highlander and

soon proved its worth in breakneck competition, much to the scream-
ing delight of both the Beacon Street debutantes and the Hanover
Street colleens who were passenger ballast for the district competing
sledders on the coast.

With the increase of these "flying skewers," the roping-off of the
coasts in the Common became a necessity for safety; and where the
pedestrian paths crossed the coasts, bridges for strollers were erected.
Youngsters from South Boston and the South End hauled their
home-made contraptions all the way to the Common to compete
with other sledders, or for the fun of stealing, as ballast, each other's
girl friends. But in spite of all safety precautions, accidents to sledders
and unwary older folks became too frequent and the fun and sport
was stopped.

The day of the doublerunner, however, continued its popularity
in South Boston, up until the eventualities of the First World War
when, because of increasing traffic, it became necessary that main
streets be plowed and sanded. South Boston in its early eras could
boast many fine slides. The principle coast began its wild slide from
atop of Dorchester Heights. Starting at G Street, the doublerunners
raced down steep East Sixth Street hill, forcing the lone "belly-
bumpers" off the coast along with pedestrians and unwary delivery
wagons, to continue on for four long city blocks, finally coming to
a stop at L Street.

First on the snow-heaped city scene was the five a.m. milkman's
clattering, bottle-rattling pung (a sleigh with boxlike body on runners)
quite often with the neighborhood foot patrolman snugly wrapped
chin-high with a horse blanket perched on the front seat along with
the driver of the horse-drawn pung. Within hours the heavy snow
was packed down solidly by pedestrians and the thousands of commercial workaday sleighs. Some, the largest of the snow-drays, had
four runners and required four horses to haul an extremely heavy
load uphill. Youngsters grabbed free rides from off the tailboards
of the house delivery pungs. Perched on the rear of the low-slung
sleigh, the gleeful kids held tightly to the pulling ropes of their
own wooden sleds that were in turn quickly filled by the free riding
small fry. Often the driver snapped at having uninvited passengers
and it was a game to see how far one could ride before there was a
snarling "git off." Part of the game was to prove one's courage.
The boy or girl who could withstand the gruff commands to "scram"

and duck the cracking whip was the "strongest of the stalwart" who took a place of special status among their "bunch." Hooking pungs was usually done in groups, and the original delivery purpose of the sleighs to cargo cases of beer, milk or groceries often became secondary to free rides for clusters of jeering youngsters, timing their leap on the rear of the pung and filled with the joy of bravery accomplished and danger dared, plus the satisfaction of nose-thumbing or snow-balling the disgruntled driver. It is not likely that a Boston man or woman ever has taken a ride more thrilling or adventurous than those hooked in the long-remembered days of their youth.

Boston's streets, because of heavy travel, would often become so ice-coated that teenage sportsmen were able to skate and play hockey on the slippery highway arenas and, being of an exceptionally fun-loving breed, they made the most of it, even to the extent that the youngsters watered down specific areas to freeze hard over. All of this provided traction for sport, but it made street conditions hazardous for the work-day horse hauling fire apparatus and pungs making groceries and milk deliveries. The large sleigh drays, piled high with hay, that were hired by groups of spooners for moonlight sleigh rides, traveled fastest on icy byways. With sleighbells jingling merrily, the spooners snugly tucked in close together under horse blankets traveled a course from City Point over to and around Franklin Park in Dorchester in the cold invigorating air of the old-fashioned Boston winter.

But here again, it wasn't all skittles, snow fun and jinglebells for Southie's boys and girls during Jack Frost's wintry reign. Young Mike or Kate's sled was often transformed into a miniature pung by simply tying on an empty Kirkman's wooden soapbox wherein the family groceries, coal and wood would be hauled off to the home. Kate would coast baby brother in the miniature pung while young Mike lugged up three flights of stairs the one hundred pound bag of weekly coal allowed a family during the winter years of the First World War. But it was all nonchalantly accepted in stride as part of a Southie kid's "bringin' up" and, besides, carrying the bag of coal up three flights kept him in good shape for the spring season ahead and the baseball diamond.

In mid-March, when the warming sun, rising higher in the sky, had dissolved the snow fort and retired the doublerunner, skates and galoshes behind the family collection of old newspapers in the cellar, a Southie's fancy turned to the prime games of the softer season ahead.   Veterans of a hard New England winter and now properly attired in less burdensome clothing, the youngsters flocked outdoors with their prized spring playthings—tops, marbles, hoops and the home-made kite.

The kites, reaching high for the clouds, heralded the end of winter and presaged the coming of spring and all the fun it would hold. First to appear on the snow-free tenement lined streets was the top. It took a special experience to saliva-moisten the tip of a waxed cord to a perfect winding—now lost and forgotten—hold the hardwood top just so and, with the experienced snap of the wrist, fling it to the asphalt pavement so that after whirling off with a startled bounce, it spun for several minutes on its metal point.

Most of the ten to twelve year olders "had their marbles" so to speak. Where it was a "down to earth game" that required finger digging in the hard packed earth for the construction of a "bunnie hole" some three or four inches deep—enough to hold a double fistful of marbles—the game was unappealing to the more fastidious lassies, and, besides, the boys played for "keepies." The expression, so common today, "he lost his marbles," first originated in South Boston.

Skipping rope, another lost skill, was the Southie girls' early spring favorite pastime. "Salt, mustard, vinegar—" was relatively easy for a trio of rope-hoppers simultaneously skipping. "Pepper" often tossed a less agile lass on her backside much to the hilarious delight of the young male, who felt it was beneath his dignity to jump rope alongside the girls but only too gladly could be persuaded to take an end of the heavy jump rope to slyly entangle their legs to toss them broadside.

Nor was race-rolling a discarded tire rim or a bicycle wheel considered sissy business. Hoop rolling required fleetness of foot, a strong arm and the courage to outshout and overcome sturdy opposition.   At the signal word "go!" the neighborhood kids, boys and girls alike, commenced the wild race around the city block. Horse and team hurriedly pulled away to one side of the course; adults hastily ducked into doorways lest the metal rim bounce over the sidewalk with the disabling fury of a cannon ball. The race usually ended up in an argumentative debate as to who did or who didn't bat another's hoop into the gutter. The dispute was finally resolved when it was discovered that an affluent member of the "bunch" had found an overlooked nickle in his jeans; whereupon he was hustled into the nearest candy store with the resulting peace offerings of chocolate covered jawbreakers being distributed.

And, as the sun rose still higher and March winds gave way to April's longer after school hours, Southie's baseball sandlots resounded with the cries of "batter up!" Down from the cellar coal bin, the fast-growing athlete gathered up his shabby collection of baseball paraphernalia that, bundled alongside his football togs, was carelessly stored last fall. Shaking the mice nest out of the catcher's mask, the aspiring young athlete began his inspectional inventory. The three "nickle rockets" lopsided and rolled around with electricians black tape were happily found serviceable. Although tape held the split handle of the bat from further disintegration, it would have to do for batting practice. The first baseman's mitt had unfortunately been nibbled away for the makings of a snug winter nest for the mice in the catcher's mask and, with nostalgic regret, it was tossed into the trash barrel. But, here again, April was the month of a birthday coming and a pointed suggestion to the "ol' man" would usually resolve the need.

Baseball, in an organized process, saw its best days beginning at the present turn of the century. Saturday afternoon fans at the M Street Grounds (now the Christopher Lee) rooted for the old "Bay Views," South Boston's first semi-professional ball club. During the early 20's, Southie's sports entrepreneur "Twilight" Bill Kelly instituted the plan of having semi-pro baseball played during twilight hours so that the workaday fan, after a hurried supper, could enjoy six or seven innings of organized ball before darkness set in. Kelly's South Boston All-Stars of an evening often attracted more fans to the M Street grounds than did Braves Field or the Red Sox's Fenway Park to their afternoon game of the same day. As a matter of fact, the Southie team played an early spring exhibition game with the National League Boston Braves and came within two runs of winning.

Twilight and his associate sports entrepreneur "Barrels" Lynch, succeeded in attracting the country's best and most colorful semi-pro teams to Southie. The attraction that drew fans from all over Boston was the Harlem Colored All-Stars, who usually had no difficulty trouncing Southie. When told that a drive over the fence into the coal yard was two bases and not a homer, the black's heavy hitters switched over to "leftie" to loft the ball clear over the bleachers. Then there were the "House of David" nine all the way from Salt

Lake City in Utah, whose attraction besides excellent ballplaying was the beards they sported. Home plate umpire Bill Brickley had difficulty calling balls and strikes on breezy days claiming poor visibility because hair got in his eyes. The Dorchester Town Team and the Contabs from Cambridge were Southie's sharpest rivals from the greater Boston area. They brought their thousand hometown rooters with them and helped fill with coins the "tin dipper" that Twilight passed under their noses between innings. Quite often, while Kelly was "collecting" and Southie's pitcher was being hit hard, Kelly (a former New England League hurler) would be rushed from out of the stands to the pitcher's box. Placing the tin dipper alongside the pitcher's mound, (never letting it out of his sight) Kelly, a leftie, would attempt to finish out the inning. He had a fast "roundhouse" that could be controlled for about an inning and a half, after which the fans gathered alongside the first base line would begin to get nervous and seek shelter behind the home plate screen leaving catcher "Tacks" Connell (another Southie immortal) to his own peril.

Besides being blessed with many oceanside and inland play pastures, Southie had an ever growing crop of impudent, sturdy youngsters eager to compete in athletics with American teams here and abroad. After a gap of 1503 years, Athens, in April of 1896, due to the initiative of athletes the world over, re-opened the ancient Olympia games. The Greeks, themselves, did not know who first started the games, and to cover up their ignorance, they said the Gods originated them. In this faraway land, 80,000 Athenians witnessed the revival of the Olympics and saw a South Boston Irish American lad win three medals.

The small American team that participated in the first games of the Olympics won 9 out of 15 track and field events. James Brendan Connolly, the Southie athlete, won the first event of the day and the first Gold Medal awarded in the Olympics for the Triple Jump (formerly known as Hop, Step, Jump) to initiate the first Olympic record, a distance of 44 feet, 11¾ inches. He went on to win the silver medal in the High Jump, 5 feet, 7¾ inches and the bronze medal for the Broad Jump, 20 feet and ½ inch.

Not officially a part of the American team at first, young Connolly worked his way "steerage" to Athens. He arrived in Greece ahead of the official BAA Team to win the first Olympic Gold Medal to be awarded to an American athlete. On a July day in 1900, in Paris, he won the Silver Medal in the Hop, Step, Jump event by placing second, this time a distance of 45 feet and 10 inches.

Connolly was honored at the White House by President Theodore Roosevelt, himself an admirer of athletes and sportsmen, where they exchanged momentos. The young athlete enlisted as a naval officer after the Spanish-American War and, later, because of his deep love for the ocean and the ways of a seafarer, he became interested in the fishermen of Gloucester. He became reknown because of his many finely detailed historical books and novels about the seven seas and the Gloucester fishermen who sailed upon them, and when the City of Gloucester historically celebrated its 300th Anniversary, Connolly was the guest of honor and deservedly feted. He ran against James Michael Curley for Congress in 1912. James Michael, who usually lampooned a political opponent, could find no fault with the gentlemanly author and years later appointed Connolly to a literary post in City Hall. Connolly returned to newspaper work during World War II as a war correspondent.

The Olympic Games are predicated on the theory that "the body of a man is of equal importance with his intellect and only by their mutual discipline and co-ordination is he glorified." James Brendan Connolly, pioneer athlete from South Boston, exemplified the Gold Medal awarded to him by adding to its worth, a life of effort and the will to win courageously.

Another trophy collector of championship calibre was Joseph Maguire, born on Castle Island off South Boston. The son of an Ordnance-Sergeant put in charge of Fort Independence in the year 1879, young Maguire began at a very early age to show ability as an oarsman. He had plenty of practice rowing back and forth from the Island to Kelly's Landing to attend the Pope School in Southie. (Dick Cushing's primary school alma mater.) He won the rowing championship of the United States in 1894. The Castle Island prodigy repeated his national conquest in 1897 and, in 1901, journeyed to Halifax to add to his list of triumphs.

Thompson's Academy, Boston's illustrious school for boys in Boston Harbor, whose *Pilgrim II* steamer also docked at Kelly's Landing, produced yet another "Island Champ" so to speak. Clarence De Mar, prodigious collector of Marathon laurels, ran the 26 mile course from Hopkinton to Boston's Back Bay to become the world's

Columbus Park — Carson Beach — Dorchester Heights

most admired and consistent Marathon winner over a space of two decades.

Another young athlete who was born on Southie's ocean-bound coast was Louise Day Hicks. As a young girl she had only to cross the beach boulevard from the house she was born and raised in to either swim M Street Beach or to train at the famous Women's L Street Baths. Training hard for an entire summer, Louise won several medals in the swimming events held at City Point. During her early college years, Louise, a devotee of good health and exercise, was bent on becoming a "lady doctor." But, she was persuaded by her father, Judge Day, to enter his office as a law clerk. Mrs. Hicks walks with an alert and graceful stride that is the reward of her youthful athletic days and of her "inheritance" so to speak.

And yet another of Southie's beloved briny sports was given a strong impetus, when under the overall leadership of Harry McDonough of Southie, a regatta with prize sailboat racing climaxed the Metropolitan District Commission's first sailing season at Pleasure Bay Lagoon off Castle Island's waters. The MDC sailing program was launched during the summer of 1972 with a fleet of 25 Kingfisher boats. More than 400 sailing enthusiasts—300 under the age of 18, signed on for boat craftsmanship.

McDonough and volunteers from the nearby South Boston Yacht Club teach the new sailors. "We teach safety first and swimming is a part of it. Sailing teaches one self reliance. Kids can learn plenty in this program. Decisions must be made instantly—lessons are learned fast."

One of yesteryear's outstanding mermaids, pride of the "L," was champion woman swimmer, Madeline Berlo (of the potato salad concocting Berlos). She was referred to as the "Modern Venus De Milo" by Dr. Sargent at whose Harvard School of Physical Culture she was a swimming instructor. Madeline and her "5 Berlo Girls" gave a series of brilliant diving exhibitions at the best theatres throughout the country. The gigantic production was especially presented at the Bowdoin Square Theatre in Boston for a command hometown audience during the week of November 13th, 1921. Described by the press as "graceful, shapely diving Venuses," the Southie girls performed in the largest tank ever erected upon any stage, holding 5500 gallons of water. Buxom Madeline, by no means skin and bones, and a little too anxious to please her L Street admirers, plunged into the enormous tank to end up in what is referred to in L Street swimming circles as a "bellyflop." Whereupon, a splashed Irish L Street brownie arose from his front-row seat and shouted out indignantly, "Gar dommit—gur'rl, if I'd knowed ye was goin' to do that, I'd 'a worn me fig leaf!"

During all summer seasons, Dorchester Bay is witness to an ever-changing marine spectacle offered by the sailing of vessels, varying in size from huge ocean liners making the turn into Boston Harbor outside of Castle Island to the smaller sailboat. Accidents occurred in the inner bay, occasioned by unskillful sail-boating. For many years a floating life-saving station, the only one of its kind in the world, cut down on harbor tragedies. With the arrival of power-driven craft, service was discontinued.

Dorchester Bay, now one of the greatest yachting centers in the country, offers natural facilities for all types of sailing with abundant moorage supplied by the shore-lined yacht clubs with long floating platforms and easy embarkment secured. Principal among them, are the Boston Yacht Club, The South Boston Yacht Club, The Columbia Yacht Club, The Puritan Canoe Club and the Mosquito Yacht Club (now demolished) then at the foot of K Street.

Boxing is to this day a prime favorite with Southie's youngsters. On rainy days, the kids would chalk out squares in their cellar club-rooms, sparring and learning the rudiments of self-defense. The young boxers, under the auspices of the Boston Parks and Recreation Department, held their 39th annual Baby Golden Gloves boxing show at the McDonough Memorial Gym. At the 1971 show, twenty-one bouts were staged in weight classes from 45 to 135 pounds, with special bouts in the 80 and 85 pound class.

South Boston's "Peres" during the early "twenties" became the most popular football team in Southie's entire sport-loving history. The club was sponsored by the Pere Marquette Council, Knights of Columbus and was first coached by Leo Daly and managed by Mike King. The team won the hearts and loyalty of Southie. Most of their games were played Sunday afternoons on the hard-packed C. J. Lee Playground at the foot of M Street, where for several years they met other top semi-pro New England elevens before capacity crowds of 10,000 or more people. The *Boston Post* in its sports page listed the pioneer team on November 7, 1921 as follows:

RE   Derby, Mooney
RT   Brady, Santry, Kennealey
RG   Collins, A. O'Brien
 C   Colman, McDonald
LG   R. O'Brien, Hurley
LT   Kirby, Knox, Carr
LE   Manning, O'Connor, Fouy
QB   Santry, McMahon, Thornton
RHB V. Plansky, O'Leary
LHB T. Plansky
FB   C. O'Brien, Flaherty

One of the finest games played by the Peres occurred on a Saturday afternoon on November 10, 1926 at Braves Field in Boston against the leaders of the National Professional Football League, the powerful Providence Steam Rollers from Rhode Island. The Providence eleven, with Gus Sonnenberg, the world's champion wrestler, in their lineup, were favored to down Southie. The Steam Rollers were called upon to show all the football mettle they possessed to stave off the fierce attack of the Southie eleven. Sonnenberg, who was famous for his "flying tackle" in the wrestling ring, found himself on the bottom of the pile more often than not. Billy O'Leary, Southie immortal, sparked his teammates with a series of brilliant end runs and the former Boston College star, Bud Dower, booted out punts that averaged 70 yards each. Carrying the ball over their opponent's goal line three times, the Peres were called back twice because of infractions. Finally, they had to concede the game to the Steam Rollers by the score of 14 to 7. The following week at the C. J. Lee Playground, the Peres resumed their fantastic winning and scoring feats by defeating the Springfield Acorns by a 54 to 0 score.

The one semi-pro club that occasionally gave the Southie eleven a rough time was the Fitton A. C. from East Boston. They drove hard, played rough and, on one of their annual Thanksgiving Day games, delighted the Eastie fans by trouncing the over-confident Peres. The St. Alphonsus A. C. from Roxbury often held their ground against Southie. On a November Sunday in 1923, the Roxbury club was holding the Peres scoreless. In the final quarter, John McClosky, Peres' star of the day, broke away to run the entire length of the field for the only touchdown of the game.

After more than a decade of gridiron victories, the Peres left the field to yet another great Southie eleven, the *Chippewas*. Composed of former sandlot stars and high school grads, the warriors delight in "sport for sport's sake." The "Chippies" claim the distinction of being the oldest and best organized football club in the Country. Time after time, a consistent winner in the Boston Park League, the team represented South Boston, when the Eastie-Southie Thanksgiving Day football classic was called off because of the 1974 school boycott. The Chippies played the strong Fitton A. C. in the East Boston Stadium to maintain a football tradition of more than seventy years.

Perched high on top of historic Dorchester Heights, South Boston High School has, since its conception at the turn of the century, produced an exceptional crop of gridiron elevens. Year after year, the school continues to lead in football standings in the Boston District League, at times scoring over 200 points before being scored upon. Winning 58-0 in one particular game at the White Stadium in Dorchester, the team rolled up 405 yards in total offense while notching its sixth victory and fifth shutout of the season. Southie outscored its opposition 232-6. Coach Crowley in his 15th year at Southie has never lost more than two games in a season.

"I don't coach to shut out everybody—maybe those shutouts meant something to the kids, but our coaching staff didn't pay any attention to it," said Crowley in explanation of the school's exuberance and Southie's traditional urge to win, and win big.

The entire recreational area of South Boston, especially thought out and planned by foresighted city fathers, proves by its rewarding existence and records of accomplishment that its youthful athletes, because of exceptional physical training and facilities, have developed leadership qualities that have profited the entire nation. One has but to see the many lithe young bodies flashing about happily on the peninsula's many beaches and playground areas to realize that in Southie the ideals of the ancient Olympic games are reborn.

CLEANLINESS OF BODY IS TRUE
REVERENCE TO GOD

L Street Bathhouse. Memorial to "Father Joe" Laporte

Over the door of the Men's L Street Bathhouse on Day Boulevard the reverential analect inspires and reminds the enterer of an obligation due to the temple of the body and to God. The authorized analect was approved by the former Mayor of Boston, the Hon. James Michael Curley in 1931 who, with the political leaders of Southie, was instrumental in having the wooden structured L, that was built in 1900, demolished and replaced with the present stone building erected in its place. Beginning with a small wooden building erected in 1865 for the purpose of "allowing men and boys to disrobe and store their clothing while enjoying their bath," the original municipally owned, free to the public institution became world famous. As early as 1951, it was estimated that over 22 million people had passed through the doors of the bathhouse.

The memorial adjacent to the famous L is a testimonial to reverential appreciation by Southie's youngsters who, by concerted efforts, gathered the wherewithal to defray the cost of the memorial perpetuating the counciling of their saintly and deceased friend "Father Joe" Laporte.

> *Do not forget those that have had charge of you, and preached God's word to you; contemplate the happy issue of the life they lived, and imitate their faith—Heb. 7:13.*

The Boy's section of the L had both name and facilities changed to "The Curley Recreation Center" in 1972. The facilities include a sauna and a well-equipped "slimnastic" exercise room for women and girls. Other activities include chess lessons (for all ages), basic sewing, crafts and music. Boy's activities: street hockey, weight lifting, boxing, pool and table tennis. A gladiator universal machine and a steam room are available for men over 16.

Curley Recreation Center — L Street Bathhouse

THE GOLDEN "ALL-OVER" TAN

(The Brownies)

The term "baths" at the famous L Street Bathhouses can be deceiving, for in its proper sense, there are no "bath" facilities, unless bathing in the ocean and a cold, fresh water shower can be construed as having had a bath. It is, however, the peculiarity of the combined advantages of salt-water swimming and the golden "all-over" sun-baths (fig leaf only in the men's and boy's sections—bikini for the ladies in their closed-off section) that have given this historic tri-sectional structure its unique reputation and appeal.

Activities in the Men's L include: volleyball, handball, horseshoes, and calisthenics. Handball, the game that requires perfect physical condition and agility, has been traditional at the "L" for six decades. When the old single, wooden-wall court was torn down, every stage of the new concrete being constructed was watched apprehensively. Every moment of lost time was lamented over by the athletes lest the courts not be completed in time for the yearly New England three-wall championship tournaments.

Frank O'Conner and his brother Neil, native Southies, were doubles champions in 1918. "Handball is something special and because of its tradition here at the 'L', it is always a great take-in." Frank rattled off a list of the old-time handball greats of yesteryear and the many Boston pros and amateur athletes that used the courts to keep in trim.

For the brownie inclined towards mental relaxation, there are checkerboard and chess designs painted on the concrete walks. The bid whist or bridge enthusiast needs only sunglasses, a deck of cards and the surface sand as seat for his sun-tanned buttocks.

The requirement that only necessitates the wearing of a fig leaf was instituted with the foresight that "all-over" exposure to the sun was healthful and that the discomfiture of sitting around in a set of damp swim trunks would be eliminated. All of which makes the recreation-

The Golden All-Over Tan – the Brownies

al features of the world famous "L" in Southie, one of the most unique of its kind and the happiest.

Long distance swimming events and aquatic sports were sponsored by the L Street Swimming Club. One of the most colorful, "the L Street to Boston Light Swim," received nationwide publicity. Contestants lined up for the endurance swim, amid cheers of thousands, begin the arduous test through chilly waters towards the distant lighthouse. Surprisingly, a large percentage finish the grueling test of endurance. American long distance swimmers, Charles Toth and Sam Richards, both conquerors of the English Channel swim, have participated in the Boston Light swim in preparation for the France to England endurance test. The experience gained at South Boston's L resulted in other participations here in America and abroad.

On record cold days, the Boston newspapers find a weird delight in publishing human interest photos of the health-conscious brownies drying off on a floating ice floe after a plunge in the frigid Dorchester Bay.

"Once the toes are in, the rest is easy," chin-chattered a blue-lip brownie kook, "you get a feeling of well-being when you get out of the water." He admitted his wife didn't like his polar bear socialities. "She sent me to see a doctor so he would tell me not to go in swimming in the winter any more," he explained as seagulls and the rest of the brownies frolicked for the photographers, "but the doctor examined me and told me to keep it up." It almost appears that the remarkable brownies indulge in this wintry practice just to tantilize snowbound New Englanders and confound the Floridians and their winter-evading Miami Beach guests.

The Three Samaritans — "May They Never Be Forgotten"

THE THREE SAMARITANS

"May They Never Be Forgotten"

Daily, thousands of hurrying motorists and strolling pedestrians pass by the memorial dedicated to three Southie lads. Surely, they must ponder to themselves at the persisting gratitude of the youth of South Boston. Every day, flowers gathered from a nearby garden, fresh with morning dew, or the floral sprays and wreaths from the biers of Southie's waked dead are placed at the base of the memorial as a constant remembrance of the three young men. *Their spirit lives on in memoriam.*

Lesson number one, in South Boston's Cardinal Cushing's curriculum of compassion can be found in the gospel of the "Good Samaritan" concerning a person who is compassionate and helpful to one in distress. (See Luke 10:30-37.)

It was a cold, wet night on Saturday, December 14, 1968, when the usual contingent of Southie teenagers headed for the Surf Ballroom at Nantasket Beach on the South Shore for their weekly dance. They were the youngsters who had graduated from the local parish and were now meeting with their young friends from neighboring communities. Upon completion of the dance, the three Southie lads, "Mike" Beatty, "Ernie" Santoro, and "Jackie" Walker volunteered their rides home to others who, they thought, were less fortunate than they. The three were boyhood friends of long standing and felt that as long as they stayed together no harm could come.

There are no eye witnesses as to what actually happened, but it is a fact that while hitch-hiking home the three encountered a disabled motorist in Hingham. With true Southie spirit, the three lads began pushing the car of the owner, even though he was heading south and their destination was north. As one of their friends remarked at the time of the tragedy "that car wasn't even going the same way they were, and most likely they wouldn't have gotten a ride even if they got it started."

Out of the dark, wet night, another motorist, not seeing the lads, hit the three of them. Two were killed instantly, the third died within hours without ever regaining consciousness. When the news of the accident reached South Boston the next morning, the entire community felt bereft. Before the sun set that day, a meeting of over thirty-five friends was held in the L Street Bathhouse where an organization was formed, officers elected, and committees appointed for one of the most spontaneous efforts the district has ever seen.

The first contributions to the memorial were those self-imposed on the original group. When others heard of the fund, there was an immediate and generous response from schools, labor organizations, businessmen and concerned individuals, all interested that the South Boston would succeed in perpetuating the memory of their deceased friends.

Securely attached to the outside wall of the South Boston High School Annex on Day Boulevard is a finely sculptured memorial that pays homage to the memory of the three youthful South Boston Samaritans.

THEIR SPIRIT LIVES ON IN MEMORIAM

This monument erected with funds voluntarily contributed by the friends and youth of this community in loving and grateful memory of "Mike" Beatty, "Ernie" Santoro, and "Jackie" Walker, who lost their lives in an accident while serving as good samaritans.

The measure of their lives was not in years. Their thoughtful friendship enriched the lives of all who knew them and as friends shared their joy and sorrows to the end of their days.

Their little nameless acts of kindness and love will serve as an inspiration and their memory a benediction.

May they rest eternally together

Dedicated December 14, 1969.

A HUMBLE BEGINNING

Birthplace of Richard Cardinal Cushing, Archbishop of Boston

(808 East Third Street, South Boston, August 24, 1895)

"I never dreamed that Providence would allow me the privilege of presiding at the installation of my successor as the Archbishop of Boston."

"I have seen it," said Richard Cardinal Cushing, "and I am glad." Amid a burst of cheers, an unprecedented wave of applause, and a stirring chorus of "Alleluias," he slowly made his way down the center aisle of the Holy Cross Cathedral in the South End of Boston.

A little boy, thoughtfully watching the aged cardinal's unsteady approach, his worn and haggard features as he slowly walked back to the church rectory, turned to his parents and asked, "Didn't he used to be young once?"

Any assessment of Richard James Cushing as a lad must take into account the influences and characteristics of the community he was born and raised in. All his youthful days in South Boston he loved gatherings of people, and associated himself with all of them.

"I identified myself with the other lads in South Boston and mixed in all their joys and actions. In those days, the boys were tough and they were strong. I was as rough as any of them, and they were pretty rough.

"They were good years," Cardinal Cushing recalled the days of his youth in the Pope School district. "We were ordinary people, poor, but comfortable. I loved my neighbors because they were neighborly. When as a boy, I was sick or lonely, they took care of me. South Boston folks are still a laboring people, born and brought up in an area which has contributed greatly to America's way of life. The people have a tremendous love and interest in one another. Protestant, Catholic, and Jewish, they are all wonderful folks who work together. There is nothing so beautiful as my South Boston."

Cardinal Cushing never sought the role that he retained for 26

Birthplace of Richard Cardinal Cushing — "A Humble Beginning"

years. Even as late as 1962, he tried to resign in an attempt to end his career in the missions of Latin America. Kindly critics on observing and becoming aware of his failing health doubted that his once strong source of energy could sustain his desires. Instead, he was encouraged by the wishes of the faithful to remain active in his beloved Boston Archdiocese where his extraordinary ability to raise prodigious funds for his Latin American missionaries and his charitable works at home prompted Bostonians of many faiths to refer to him as the "Cardinal of Charity."

As he aged, it was apparent that his faltering health became a Christlike cross for him to bear. At times he would however, indulge himself in the luxury of being "crotchety," particularly of those that would be self-seeking or too demanding of his time and energies. His style of delivering homilies faltered. Spoken in a slowing manner, his nasal, rasping South Boston accentuated oratory would drone on rather interminable, and at times boringly. Yet withal, his courage, mentality—and above all, his strong religious fervor remained firm and steadfast.

"Know your faith! Live your faith! and recognize the faith of others!" admonished Boston's extraordinary Ordinary that declared himself an ecumenist when he became Archbishop. Son of a South Boston Irishman, he shattered the barricades of religious prejudice in his beloved Boston. He watched his flock of diverse nationalities overcome economic and political ostracism and assume their fair share of governmental offices. He warned Catholics that it was a "grave sin against God to succumb to racial hatred and bigotry." A practical man, he understood that people must be led—not pushed, punished unfairly, nor they or their property abused.

". . .Let this land—and all lands—move forever under Thy guidance and through his leadership to New Frontiers in peace, progress and prosperity." The invocation of President Kennedy's inaugural was delivered by Cardinal Cushing. The election of John F. Kennedy as 35th President of the United States dispelled the myth that a Catholic could not attain the nation's highest office. Cardinal Cushing had publicly labeled young Kennedy as the next President of the United States, two years before his nomination and election.

Only the Cardinal's once huge energy had obscured the truth about how long, and how seriously he had been ill. For years he had fought off migraine headaches, ulcers, asthma and emphysema. The latter two so debilitating that he had to keep oxygen at his bedside. When he died at the age of 75, cancer had so ravished his 6-ft. frame that he wasted from 200 lbs. to a mere 140 lbs.

Confirmed in this faith, we commend this valient newsmaker to the history books, this holy man, this zealous priest, this uncommon prelate we commend to the God who gave joy to his youth, the Christ who consoled his age, the angels and saints with whom he now shares eternal life, undying love!

John Cardinal Wright

At his bedside with his personal physician, Dr. Richard Wright, the brother of John Cardinal Wright, were his brother John and his two sisters, Mrs. Anna Francis and Mrs. Mary Pierce. Speaking for the family Mrs. Pierce bravely and simply said the few words to which brevity added a halo. . . .He was always wonderful to people—he will be missed by everybody. Archbishop Medeiros was at his bedside when he died. His death had to come, for he could not fight on forever.

Ut Cognoscant Te — That They May Know Thee, O Lord

Portiuncula Shrine

UT COGNOSCANT TE

"THAT THEY MAY KNOW THEE, O LORD"

(circa 1967)

Saint Coletta's School for Exceptional Children, Hanover, Mass.

"I request that I be buried in the Portiuncula Shrine located at Saint Coletta by the Sea in Hanover, Massachusetts."

Fittingly, Richard Cardinal Cushing was buried on a Saturday, November 7, 1970 in a simple crypt in St. Coletta's "facing the children" as he so desired. A few days after his burial, Sister Shawn, O.S.F., superintendent of the school, announced a name change. . . Saint Coletta's School for Exceptional Children in Hanover, where Cardinal Cushing is buried, will be renamed in honor of the Cardinal, the man to whom the children meant so much." Immediate approval for the name change came from Archbishop Humberto Medeiros.

Sister Shawn observed that the children had given her the idea for the change, since they remembered so well the visits the Cardinal made there when health permitted.

Inside the crypt, on a little hillside, buried under the red bolero of a Cardinal's Coat of Arms lay the body of a dedicated priest from South Boston.